T0146724

FIRING THE
YOUTHS TO DAWN

FIRING THE YOUTHS TO DAWN

ORUONYE SAMUEL

To order additional copies of this book, contact:
Xlibris
1-888-795-4274
www.Xlibris.com
Orders@Xlibris.com
736708

CONTENTS

Chapter 1

IDENTITY CRISIS

The world of today is not the world of yesterday because yesterday comes before today and tomorrow is tougher than today. therefore the preparation of today determines the success or failure of tomorrow. Hence, we the present youths of today must understand the role to play and to know how to play it and also to know how we might overcome the possible challenges that might arise in the nearest future. But we cannot do anything without understanding what we want to do or the problems that we are facing that has been the reason of the failures of many youths of today. So in this book, we shall be discussing the possible crisis of the youths of today and how to overcome them.

This book has been written by the inspiration of God Almighty and has been ordered to be prints in several languages as to enhance the understanding of many, to free many from several kinds of bondages, to empower many and also preserve many. Therefore believe all that is written in this book and practice it with confidence and you shall surely testify.

THE Bible said that God create man in his own image in GENESIS chapter1. In genesis God made man and woman in his own image and likeness therefore man is equal to man and not God.

Identity crisis is the very crisis the world has suffered for ages now but the ignorance here is that God has made man to be perfect but they are filled with many inventions.

In this topic we shall be dealing with the following; Race, Religion

1] RACE;

RACE is one of the major crisis the world is facing now because the devil has possess the minds of the children of GOD in making them believe that they are better superior than others. Now in

1cor3vs3-9

3:For ye are yet carnal: for whereas there is among you envying, and strife, and divisions, are ye not yet carnal, and walk as men?

4 For while one saith, I am of Paul; and another, I am of Apollos; are ye not carnal?

5 Who then is Paul, and who is Apollos, but ministers by whom ye believed, even as the Lord gave to every man?

6 I have planted, Apollos watered; but God gave the increase.

7 So then neither is he that planted anything, neither he that watereth; but God that giveth the increase.

8: Now he that planted and he that watereth are one: and every man shall receive his own reward according to his labour.

9:For we are labourers together with God: ye are God's husbandry, ye are Gods building.

Paul was writing to the Corinthians and said; for while one saith I am of Paul and the other saith I am of Apollo, is ye not carnal? Then he said who is Paul and who is Apollo? But the minister for whom ye believed even as GOD gave to everyman. Finally he said ''I have planted Apollo watered but God gave the increase.

Now if God gave the increase, there is no point of envying because is truly not in the power of man but GOD, therefore there should not be division among us nor one say am of catholic and the other say am of Pentecostal. So whether black or white, rich or poor, sick or strong there should not be division nor envying or strife because to everyman gave him power to subdue, and have dominion over everything that is not glorifying God in his or her life.

Please understand that the Bible said in

Romans9vs15-16:

For he said to Moses, I will have mercy on whom I will mercy, and I will have compassion on whom I will have compassion.

16: so then it is not of him that willeth, nor of him that runneth, but of God that sheweth mercy.

So is the mercy of GOD that places every one of us where we are and where we should be. Therefore let us be just in judgment, not taking side because of color or wealth because it is Gods mercies that take us to where we want to be or where we are now.

Identity crisis is a huge crisis that grows every day because the devil has disguise himself in it and use it to cause a lot of problems in the world today especially in the lives of the youths. Please understand that whatever problem you see on earth today is been cause as a result of the manifestation of the devils in the lives humans because the Bible said in

John10v10:

For the thief cometh not, but to steal, and to kill, and to destroy; I am come that they might have life, and that they might it more abundantly.

So the work of the devil is to kill, steal and to destroy therefore there is nothing good about the devil. The devil has used identity to cause lots of harms to this world especially in the lives of the youths today. First the devil makes them not to believe in themselves, not to believe that the future is good, not to believe their government, which eventually makes them feel rejected in the society even when the opposite is the case. the devil bring unnecessary fear upon the youths which bring about evil accomplishment by the youths. The devil has used identity crisis to kill a lot of youths and children because he has make them not to know that they possess the spirit of Almighty God whom all things summit because the psalmist said in

Psalms24v1

The earth is the Lord's, and the fullness thereof; the world, and they that dwell therein.

The earth is of the Lord and the fullness thereof.....and God cannot lie so if the Bible is true which is because in

john1v1....*the word was God.*

So if the word was God himself than we should apply them in our daily lives and not to kill because of money, power, resentments because the earth is of the LORD'S.

It is very good to understand every position we find ourselves in our daily lives. Therefore, it is a good thing for the youths of today to realize their positions on earth. Youths should understand that the strength of the world is in their hands because the military of any Nation is 90percent youths. Therefore understand how important you are in the society as to be able to accept and reject certain offers in your life. The Almighty God has given you all you need to be all you need because the Bible said in

Psalm82v5-6.5 *They know not, neither will understand; they walk on in darkness: all the foundation of the earth are out of course*

6 I have said, ye are gods; and all of you are the of the Most High

They know not neither will they understand ...I have said ye are gods and all of you are children of the Most High.

Now the question here is what does gods do? If God himself called us gods than we are gods, because snake begot snakes, dog begot dogs and GOD begot gods. He said "all of you are the children of the Most High he didn't say some of you are the children of the Most High nor did he say some are the children of the rich or poor but all of you are the children of the Most High which means everybody in this world. whether black or white, rich or poor, French or Russia are all children of the Most High but the sad news is that so many doesn't have this knowledge so they die like men and fall like one of the prince because they know not.

So the question remains what does gods do? In Genesis God created all things in this world and brought them to Adam to know what he will call them and whatever Adam calls them God accept it. Remember that Adam was the last creation of GOD but it was him that was made in the image of God. It means that man can also create and recreate because the creator of all things is his father. The animal has the gift of reproduction but not creation, thus, man was made above all things that were made on the surface of the earth because he was an image of God. Therefore as a youth, we have the capacity to create our future by accepting the will of God in our lives. We can make our future colorful by the will of God.

Please understand that God has place us above limitations and worry, above principalities and powers, above pains and sorrows, lift us up above poverty and wants, above sickness and diseases, and above all things. You can be what you want to be irrespective of your race, whether white or black because God is one.

For a long time now, the world is still trying to solve the problem of racism and have not really solved it because I believed they have not really discovered the secrets about racism. In

Matthew12v29:

Or else how can one enter into a strong man's house, and spoil his goods, except he first bind the strong man? and then he will spoil his house.

Jesus while speaking to his accusers said"....or else how can one enter into a strong mans house and spoil his goods except he first bind the strong mans and then he will spoil his house. For someone to solve a problem permanently and correctly, the person has to identify the curse of the problem before looking for the solutions. For instance, if someone is sick of malaria, and eventually goes to a clinic for checkup, the Doctor wills first carryout test on the patient before knowing what to do. so is racism and every problem upon the surface of the earth.

WHAT IS RACISM? Some definitions of racism are similar in many ways that means the same. One of the definition states that Racism is discrimination of one's race and the belief that one's race is superior to the other. Therefore racism is a carrier of hatred, conflicts, and pride between different races. But with my little experience with God I have been privilege to know the product of the devil because the bible said in

John10v10

For the thief cometh not, but to steal, and to kill, and to destroy; I am come that they might have life, and that they might it more abundantly.

The devil is only to kill and destroyed. But the question is, in what means does devil carryout his devices? What are the products of the devil? Because the bible said "by their fruits ye shall know them. So what are the fruits of the devil? The answers to these questions are stated below

Here are some of the fruits of the monster called devil

{1} **Hatred**
{2} **Pride**
{3} **Conflicts**

Now these three words form racism and I was made to understand that a man's word is how he is even the bible said that in

John1v1: *In the beginning was the Word, and the Word was with God, and the Word was God.*

The Word was God and also the word hatred, pride, conflicts is devils. Therefore I define racism as devil in action. Racism in other hand is the craftiness of the devil in the kingdom of men. So racism is the work of the devil because it deals with pride, Hatred and Conflicts. Now in **Genesis2v1-25** so all things that God created was good and also in

Psalms82v5-6.

They know not, neither will understand; they walk on in darkness: all the foundations of the earth are out of course

6 I have said, ye are gods; and all of you are the of the Most High

Therefore understand that you are a child of the Most High so are others who believed. So nothing makes us superior to others or less superior because all are children of the Most High. If am rich now does not mean another will not be rich, for God gave every man grace that is sufficient for him. So understand that the difference between a ripe pawpaw and the unripe is time because with time the unripe will be ripe. Therefore boast not thy self for tomorrow for thou knowest not what a day bring forth

Proverb27v1

Boast not thyself of tomorrow; for thou knowest not what a day may bring forth.

I pray that the three spirits of the devil that brings about racism on earth be destroy in the lives of the people in the name of Jesus Christ Amen. Every forms of deceit from the devil to curse conflicts in lives of the youths I command it to be destroy in Jesus name Amen.

Romans9v15-16.

For he said to Moses, I will have mercy on whom I will mercy, and I will have compassion on whom I will have compassion.

16 so then it is not of him that willeth, nor of him that runneth, but of God that sheweth mercy.

So is the mercy of God that matters. If there be mercies of God in our lives give glory to God and not to use the free gifts of God to oppress people. Some years back, I had a friend who I love and we were very close in such that people thought that we are brother but as time goes by things began to change for good to him. So God bless him materially and after that he no longer recognized me anymore. I ran into him one day and I called him but he didn't respond and I tried several times to get him back but to no avail maybe because he now goes by a car and I don't. This is pride and is very dangerous and is also racism because pride is found in it. In

2chr20v1-17

It came to pass after this also, that the children of Moab, and the children of Ammon, and with them beside the Ammonites, came against Jehoshaphat to battle....

5 And Jehoshaphat stood in the congregation of Judah and Jerusalem, in the house of the LORD, before the new court...

10 And now, behold, the children of AMMON AND Moab and mount seir, whom thou wouldest not let Israel invade, when they came out of the land of Egypt, but they turned from them, and destroyed them not...

12 O our God, wilt thou not judge them? For we have no might against this great company that cometh against us; neither know we what to do: but our eyes are upon thee,

14....came the Spirit of the LORD in the midst of the congregation;

15....thus saith the LORD unto you, Be not afraid nor dismayed by reason of this great multitude; for the battle is not your but God's

17 ye shall not need to fight in this battle: set yourselves, stand ye still, and see the salvation of the LORD with you,.....

Now three nations came up against Israel {Judea} the children Moab, Ammon and mount seir . these nations that came against Israel was driven by pride because they feel that they are superior maybe by numbers or ammunitions or that their gods is better, therefore they came up against Judea {conflicts} but Judea gather together and ask for help from the Lord **2chr20v5-7** so in verse **20** the king said...**believe in the Lord your God so shall ye establish and believe in his prophet so shall ye prosper.**

Remember also that in

john1v1

In the beginning was the WORD, and the WORD was with God, and the WORD was God.

Therefore believe only in the Lord, not in your own knowledge or understanding because the bible said in

1cor2v5

That your faith should not stand in the wisdom of men, but in the power of GOD.

2chr20v22-23

And when they began to sing and to praise, the LORD set ambushment against the children of Ammon, Moab, and Mount seir, which were come against Judah; and they were smitten. 23......and when they have made an end of the inhabitants of seir, every one helped to destroy another.

So my friends do not believe in your riches or the military of your Nation or the medical equipments but believe in the power of God. Now the bible said that God set ambushments against the children of Ammon, Moab and Mount seir which came up against Judea and they were smitten.

So there confidence failed and they were all dead. Therefore put not your confidence in anything that is not GODs. Now the children of Moab, Ammom, Mount seir died that day because they were ignorant of the works of the devil. They fail to recognize the three spirits of the devil which has done much harm to this world. What stir up that battle was pride, hatred, envy which is the products and fruits of the Devil? This is the plans of the devil that men should die like men, and that men should not know the original purpose of God in their lives and that is why Jesus said in

> **John 10v10**; *the thief commeth not to steal, but for to steal, kill and destroy: I have come that they might have life and that they might have it more abundantly.*

The thief cometh to kill, steal and to destroy and the children of Moab, Ammon and Mount seir could not understand the tricks of the devil.

Please understand that the devil knew that God will fight for the children of Judea because he knew it is written in exodus14v14 that the Lord will fight for you and ye shall hold your peace but he Satan wanted the children of Moab, Ammon, Mount seir to perish which is his primary mission on earth [to kill steal and to destroy} which also he has used to kill a lot of people in this world today. I realize that youths are always the target of the devil because through some of them he devil carry out his wicked activities. Though it was not so from the beginning but the devil has turned the heart of father against the son and mother against the daughter making them not to know there true self.

Please understand that the knowledge of God is very important in our lives because through Him we have eternal life. The bible said ''I am the way the truth and the life no one comes to the father except through me

John10v9;

I am the door: by me if any man enter in, he shall be saved, and shall go in and out, and find pasture.

So is only through Jesus that we have eternal life and also with Him our lives is guarantee.

Identity crisis has become severe in the world today and it is affecting the youths more and more than one can imagine because now terrorism is taking much lives every day. I pray that God should open the eyes of people and that governments should see reasons why it is important to add more efforts in developing the youths all over the world even now and the generation to come.

Please understand that racism gave birth to terrorism. Terrorism as we know is racism in disguise. In Nigeria in the 2009,south-south part of the nation, a group of young youths rise up and called themselves militants, first we had kidnap cases especially foreigners and later prominent men of the society. But before then some people had died as a result of one thing or the other. Now the question here is what can possibly curse these unrests in the south-south? Their reasons, was that to them the government is not doing to their expectations because to them the Niger delta was forsaken, no development, no employment and yet they have oil spillage from some oil companies and government. They believe that the northerners are proving superior or the development is more in the northern states or even think that the northerner are abusing the power by making them of no value or maybe because they are minority. But while all these are going on, there are blood sheds. Lives are been taken, materials are been loss, properties are been destroyed and finally amnesty was given and peace came but the lives that was loss never came till date. That is racism not just terrorism because if it is not racism what stop them from killing their own sisters or brothers or their villagers but they did not because they are all in one league, race or belief that either they are superior or inferior so they must curse trouble at the expense of others; why because hatred is found in their hearts. Can someone plant a bomb inside himself without been consume with hatred, envy and jealousy? Can someone bomb a church or mosque without been consume with hatred? Can someone run into a market place with an explosive substance without believing that he is doing what seen right to him? Therefore I am awakening the minds of the youths of this world, where ever we are or whoever we are to understand who they are, that we are the image of God and not the devil therefore understand what the bible said; let none of these things be found in you.

Some year back, someone came to me and said "Samuel do you remember victor I said yea how about him? And he said victor is dead he was a cultist in his school. To me I thought maybe he was hired to do a job on the process he was kill. A youth privilege to be in school [university} was kill maybe for little money. If he had knew that that day will be his last he wouldn't have gone out that day. If had realize that GOD LOVES him, I don't think he would have be part of any cult that does evil.

Some people think that they are the owner of their lives forgotten that the earth is the Lords. Some point in my life someone came to me and ask "why are you always calling God at all time? That for her she don't believe in God because there is no GOD and if there is God that cares, her step father wouldn't have force her to bed which resulted to pregnancy and finally make her a prostitute but I said to her, God is real and He is merciful and kind always ready to forgive only accept that you have sin against him so I preach to her from **James4v1-3**

1   *From whence come wars and fighting among you:? Come they not hence, even of your lusts that war in your members?*
2   *Ye lust and have not: ye kill and desire to have and cannot obtain, ye fight and war yet ye have not because ye ask not*
3   *ye ask, and receive not, because ye ask amiss, that ye may consume it upon your lusts.*

at the end she had some peace because I sense it though three days earlier she has been sick that the treatment wasn't responding so in that conversation I asked her if she now believed that God can heal her and she said yes so I prayed for her and the next morning she was very strong and I asked her as soon as we finish greeting the next day, do you now believe that there is God? She smiled. Therefore try God He will never fail.

I always tell people that there is no incurable sickness. Yes not one, not when Jesus is alive **1thes1v5** *For our gospel came not unto you in word only, but also in power, and in the Holy Ghost, and much* *assurance; as ye know what manner of men we were among you for your sake.*

Now, is not just the word but also the power of God which can do all things and also in the b**ook of luke1v37 the bible said**" *For with God nothing shall be impossible.*

luke1v45

Blessed is she that believed: for there shall be a performance of those things which were told her from the Lord.

Therefore nothing on earth is impossible only believed. So believe in the LORD, again in **JOHN11V40** Jesus said to Martha **"said I not unto thee, that, if thou wouldest believe, thou shouldest see the glory of God?"**

So believe is all you need to get all you want from GOD here on earth.

Some time ago a friend of mine went to the village to sat for an examination; I don't know what really came up that brought envy upon him so they struck him with a sickness that did not allow him to continue with the examination. the sickness was very grievous so he return to the city and was taken to the hospital by his parents but wasn't responding to treatments then fortunately I saw him with his mother returning from the hospital then I said to him" ah my friend what happened to you? For you look so tried and weak. He would not reply me verbally only open his hands as a sign of "I don't know". Then I ask him to see me as soon as he is free because I perceive that the mother is tired of that illness through the look on her face. Few hours later he came to me and the Holy Ghost told me to give him sprite drink to drink, then I asked him what I can offer him but he said nothing and I asked why? And he said he will vomit it for whatever enters his mouth comes out immediately.

First I preach to him about faith because it is almost impossible to receive anything from God without faith then persuade him to take something and he accepted to take sprite and after that I prayed with him a short prayer, the next day I saw him with a ball and I asked him what he is doing with the ball? And he said that he is going to play football. This was the same person that wouldn't eat nor stand for an hour is now fit to play football. So God can used anybody to carry out his majestically works on earth only believe.

I want the youths to understand who they are that they are through the mercies of God has the power to do all things.

1thess5v14,15

now we exhort you, brethren, warn them that are unruly, comfort the feebleminded, support the weak, be patience towards all men.

15 see that none render evil for evil unto any man; but ever follow that which is good, both among yourselves, and to all men.

Therefore, do not be deceived by the devil and his agents which does nothing but to bring destruction and confusion upon man kinds. I want them to realize their status in Christ Jesus that they are not tugs or assassin nor suicide bombers, even election machineries and all other evil that has been found in the lives of some youths today.

It is important that youths of this earth understands that they are peculiar people according to the word of the Lord in

1peter2v9

But ye are a chosen generation, a royal priesthood, an holy nation. A peculiar people; that ye should shew forth the praises of him who hath called you out of darkness into his marvelous light.

So I want the youths to have the mentality that truly they are more than what they think of themselves, they are a chosen generation and a royal priesthood. Therefore, show forth the praises of GOD who had create us in his own image and likeness.

Now God wants all people of God to arise and shine even as He had said in

Isaiah60v1

Arise, shine; for thy light is come and the glory of the LORD is risen upon thee.

Therefore it is our duty to arise and shine because our light has truly come. I pray that every plans of the devil to abort the plans of God in our lives is destroyed in Jesus name Amen.

Arise because the glory of God is risen upon you. You are designed for greatness not to die a pauper nor be a bomber of churches and places, not to be a racist. Understand that you are not a failure; you are specially made for glory, never to be poor nor Assassin. Have value for your life because you are a prince in heaven and a god on earth, a conqueror of battles, a good record breaker, a king over devils, an ambassador of Christ on earth. These are what you are. It is written in the book of life in

Luke4v18-19:

The spirit of the Lord is upon me, because he hath anointed me to preach the gospel to the poor; he hath sent me to heal the brokenhearted, to preach deliverance to the captives, and recovering of sight to the blind, to set at liberty them that are bruised

19 To preach the acceptable year of the Lord.

luke10v19:

Behold, I give unto you power to tread on serpents and scorpions, and over all the powers of the enemy: and nothing shall by any means hurt you.

So that is who we are physically and spiritually in the LORD. Therefore have it mentally. I pray for you today every diverter of your blessing is curse with a curse in Jesus name Amen. I pray that any devil or his agents that will make you not to fulfill your destiny or the purpose of God in your life be consume by the fire of the Holy Ghost in Jesus name Amen. Please note that ye are the light of the world according to the bible in the book of **matthew5v13,14**: but the light cannot shine without acknowledging the true source Jesus Christ in our lives.

Ye are the salt of the earth: but if the salt has lost his savour, wherewith shall it be salted? It is good for nothing, but be cast out, and to be trodden under the feet of men.

14, ye are the light of the world. A city that is set on an hill cannot be hid.

so my friend, do not loss your savor to the devil rather rise and shine, you cannot afford to be hidden, nor die without achieving your God given purpose on earth because the bible said in

jeremiah29v11.

For I know the thoughts that I think towards you, saith the LORD, thoughts of peace, and of evil, to give you an expected end.

So don't be afraid to start because there is a protection for you.

Psalm91v1-16

1: He that dwelleth in the secret place of the most High shall abide under the shadow of the Almighty.

2: I will say of the LORD, He is my refuge and my fortress: and my God; in him will I trust.

3: Surely he shall deliver thee from the snare of the fowler, and the noisome pestilence.

4: He shall cover thee with his feathers, and under his wings shalt thou trust: his truth shall be thy shield and buckler

5: Thou shall be afraid for the terror by night; nor for the arrow that flieth by day;

6: Nor for the pestilence that walketh in darkness; nor for the destruction that wasteth at noonday.

7: A thousand shall fall at thy side, and ten thousand at thy right hand; but it shall not come nigh thee.

8: Only with thine eyes shalt thou behold and see the reward of the wicked.

9: Because thou hast made the LORD, which is my refuge, even the most High, thy habitation;

10: There shall no evil befall thee, neither shall any plague come nigh thy dwelling.

11: For he shall give his angels charge over thee, to keep thee in all thy ways.

12: They shall bear thee up in their hands, lest thou dash thy foot against a stone.

13: Thou shalt tread upon the lion and adder: the young lion and dragon shalt thou trample under feet.

14: Because he hath set his love upon me, therefore will I deliver him: I will set him on high, because he hath known my name.

15: He shall call upon me, and I will answer him: I will be with him in trouble; I will deliver him, and honour him.

16: With long life will I satisfy him, and shew him my salvation.

Also in the book of **isaiah45v1-5**

1 THUS saith the LORD to his anointed, to Cyrus, whose right hand I holden, to subdue nations before him; and I will loose the loins of kings, to open before him the two leaven gates; and the gates shall not shut;

2: I will go before thee, and make the crooked places straight: I will break in pieces the gates of brass, and cut in sunder the bars of iron:

3: And I will give thee the treasures of darkness, and hidden riches of secret place, that thou mayest know that I the LORD, which called by thy name, am the God of Israel.

4: For Jacob my servant's sake, and Israel mine elect, I have even called thee by thy name: I have surnamed thee, though thou hast not known me:

5: I am the LORD, and there is none else, there is no God beside me: I girded thee, though thou hast not known me:

So don't be afraid to quit your evil ways and make it right with your God now. Some people don't want to give their life to Christ because they are afraid to lose their boy/girl friends remember what the bible said in

job22v21-28.

Acquaint now thyself with him, and be at peace: thereby good shall come unto thee.

22: Receive, I pray thee, the law from his mouth, and lay up his words in thine heart.

23: If thou return to the Almighty, thou shalt be built up, thou shalt put away iniquity far from the tabernacles.

24 then shalt thou lay up gold as dust, and the gold of O-phir as the stones of the brooks.

25 Yea, the Almighty shall be thy defence, and thou shalt have plenty of silver.

26 For then shalt thou have thy delight in the Almighty, and shalt lift up thy face unto God.

27: Thou shalt make your prayer unto him, and he shall hear thee, and thou shalt pay thy vows.

28 Thou shalt also decree a thing, and it shall be established unto thee: and the light shall shine upon thy ways.

A 22year old girl once told me that her life doesn't have any value and I asked her why will she say that and she said that men doesn't respect her, and her own friends doesn't value her maybe is because the kind of work she does and that she is also tired of this world that several times in her life she has contemplated suicide. When her story was ended I realize that she was the enemy of herself because from her story she desired something but don't know how to get it. And because she doesn't know how to get it,then decided to be someone else. She never believed starting small or even in herself. So she ended up been a prostitute. Often times we find ourselves in such situations like Depressions, Emotional pains, Abuses and lots more. but what matters is our ability to control them. Though sometime it is curse by anger, greed and lust of the flesh. But where can comfort come? In Christ Jesus through his Word in the bible because is only the bible that transforms, other books informs. Anger, greed and lusts are the ways the devil works on the ignorance of the youths because he knew that many don't know what they possess.

She wants to be someone else that is one of her problem; she does not know what she possesses. The bible said that greater is in me than he that is in the world; therefore greater is in every believer than he that is in the world, and what is the world? world simply means the system of control because there is movie world, music world, there are several worlds. Now they that are in the music world controls the music, also movie control movies. Therefore be who you are, and who are you? You are a child of God because of the bible said in **psalm82vs6**

They know not, neither will understand; they walk on in darkness: all the foundation of the earth are out of course.

6 I have said, ye are gods; and all of you are the of the Most High.

Understand that we are gods therefore we are expected to have dominion over everything around us, not desiring other things from someone when we have the power to get beyond the person. Don't desire to be like someone else because of the outlook of the person or what the person has acquired maybe fame or reputation but desired the grace of that person not the person because when we desire the grace and possibly have it, it will add to the ones we already had but first we must know what we want because some don't know what they really want. I was asking someone what he wants from God and he said money and I asked him what he will do with the money if God gives him? For over 30 minutes he could not answer that simple question. It simply means that he did not need money. Please note, not all that scream peace actually wanted it. So you must know what you want before getting it. I desire the grace upon Bennyhims, Billy Graham and pastor Adeboye of the Redeem Christian church of God Nigeria because I love what God is doing in their lives and I want God to do more with me, I don't want to be like them but to receive the grace upon them because I know I can't be like them but myself but if I want to be like them it means that my creation by God was in vain because these men of God discovered the purpose of God in their lives also teach us to discover ours so why should one desired to be someone else when God has loaded us with his goods and favors and also with unfailing promises because in

hebrews10v23

Let us hold fast the profession of our faith without wavering;(for he is faithful that promise;)

and the bible said in *Jere29v11.*

For I know the thoughts that I think towards you, saith the LORD, thoughts of peace, and of evil, to give you an expected end.

A thought to bring us to our expected end, so what is your expected end? Heaven!, To show forth the praises of God, to have dominion over sickness and diseases, to be far above principalities and powers, to be rich, heaven is indeed the expected end of every living creature on earth, it is important that every man labor for it because whether bishop, pastors, pope, elders, pagans, cultist and Muslim will all appear before the judgment seat of God.

2corinth8v9.

For ye know the grace of our Lord Christ, that though he was rich, yet for your sakes he became poor, that ye through his poverty might be rich.

Therefore it is important that we understand who we really are and not what we are not. Youths these days want the government to do everything for them which cannot be possible. Some area in some part of the world, the youth's believed that the government is not doing or meeting their expectations, therefore some choose to be thieves, while some cause problems to the masses. It is obvious that the government cannot do all things for the people because every one is the government including the youths. So there are things the youths can do for themselves, and that is, believing God and his prophets according to the **2chro20vs20**

...Believe in the LORD your God, so shall ye be established; believe his prophets, so shall ye prosper.

Therefore, believing in God and his prophets makes us prosper. So we can prosper with or without the government .I pray today that any spirit of the devil making the youths not to prosper be destroyed in Jesus name Amen.

In 2013 in the month of April I went into an office to preach, it happens that it was a coupon house {lotto} office. Then, I saw a young man and I said to him "am not condemning you but what you are doing is not proper. How can you seat sit here and expect manna from heaven without putting yourself to work? Then he said to me ".there is no work that can pay him that much as the coupon. That he played and won often so there is no point of disturbing himself working because he has a work already. To him gambling is now a work. So the question is, if there is no money to play or luck possibly ran out of him what will be his next move? Or if the company of that lotto decides to close down what will be next? Was it not a man like him that discovered that same game they used in gambling which became his means of livelihood? Will a servant ever remain a servant? Doesn't he desire to be a master someday? That is the case of some of the youths in Nigeria, Wanting to excel without hard work. Even Jesus had to go to His father for the disciples to carry on. So the question is when will the youths be the masters of themselves? Always looking towards their uncles, parents or relations for help is not the best part but looking towards God. In the bible said in **1cor2v5**

> **That your faith should not stand in the wisdom of men,**
> **but in the power of God**

Also the bible also said woe to any man that put his trust on a man. Please note that no man was born with money nor did God create money but it was man's wisdom through the grace of God .This means that man can create so you too can create something that can bring money rather than giving a chance to the devil. I pray for you today, every good thoughts of heart be made manifest in Jesus name Amen also I pray that the spirit of good inventions come upon you now in Jesus name Amen.

Positive minds bring positive things and negative minds also bring negative things. You cannot live a positive life with a negative mind. Anything other than God is negative because there are only two forces on earth, God and Satan, and the greatest is God which is positive.

Please understand that the decision we make today has the power to build us or destroy us. Therefore take a good decision today to impact lives in your society, Nations, Schools and anywhere we find ourselves because God has called us into his marvelous light.

Finally, racism is a means which the devil has used to defraud the world by making them think that they are superior to others which bring malice upon them and also causing a lot of pains to the world. Therefore understand that all are the children of the Most High irrespective of color, language or abilities. I pray that every spirit of the devil among the youths of today be destroyed and put to shame in Jesus name Amen

RELIGION

The bible said in **Psalm 150v6**

Let everything that hath breath praise the LORD. Praise ye the LORD.

The above verse implies that religion should not be a problem to mankind, religion as we know has been a problem for the past few decays and till today the problem has not be solved.

Now the questions are,

1. Should religion be a threat? Is God many? Who is the true God? What does he require from man? These questions will be answered, including can man fight for God when he is the Almighty? At the end of this, man shall know whether it is right to fight, kill, destroyed or to praise and worship God and be at peace with all men, I pray that God gives us the wisdom to understand his ways in our lives in Jesus name Amen.

Should religion be a threat? NO, Religion is an act of worship not a threat to mankind. In **Leviticus 26v1-3**

Ye shall make you no idols nor graven image, neither rear you up a standing image, neither shall ye set up any image of stone in your land, to bow down unto it: for am the LORD your God.

2:Ye shall keep my Sabbaths, and reverence my sanctuary: I am the LORD.

3: If ye walk in my statutes, and keep my commandments, and do them;

then 4

Then I will give you rain in due season, and the land shall yield her increase, and the trees of the field shall yield their fruits.

Exodus 23v25-26

And ye shall serve the LORD thy God, and he shall bless thy bread, and thy water; and I will take sickness away from the midst of thee.

26: There shall nothing cast their young, nor be barren, in thy land: the number of thy days I will fulfill.

Now religion is nothing but worship of God or a belief of any kind. Therefore the world should beware of what they worship, the bible had said in the book of

Leviticus 26 v 1.

Ye shall make you no idols nor graven image, neither rear you up a standing image, neither shall ye set up any image of stone in your land, to bow down unto it: for am the LORD your God.

Understand that there is no other God then the Lord Jesus Christ. The youths of today has suffered because of this, because some believes are different to the other, and in all, it bring trouble to the world. Religion should not be a problem because there is only one LORD. That at the mention of his name every knee must bow and every tongue must confess that Jesus is Lord to the glory of the father.

Phillipians2v10v11.

That at the name of Jesus every knee should bow, of things in heaven, and things in earth, and things under the earth;

11: And that every tongue should confess that Jesus Christ is Lord, to the glory of God the father.

Please note that Jesus Christ is the only way to salvation and also through him is the victory over all devils like sickness and lack, bad dreams and lots more. Bible said in the book of **mark16v15-18**

And he said unto them, go ye into all the world, and preach the gospel to every creature.

16: He that believeth and is baptized shall be save; but he that believeth not shall be danmed.

17: And these signs shall follow them that believe; in my name shall they cast out devils; they shall speak with new tongues;

18: They shall take up serpents; and if they drink any deadly things, it shall not hurt them; they shall lay hands on the sick, and they shall recover.

I must confess, since I acquaint with Jesus, demons has been very disappointed by works of god in my life because by the name of Jesus Christ many has been healed and delivered. So anybody can do it if he wants. But first he must believe in his heart, confess it with his mouth and that is it.

Many youths today lack this true Knowledge; they think that miracles are for the pastors, priests, bishops alone. Everyone is eligible to do more miracles than the Pastors. Yes! You are eligible if you believed in your heart. So believed is what it takes. I pray that the zeal of God and the spirit of believe come upon you in Jesus name.

Some parts of the world go to Nigeria to receive healing from God and many thought it is magic. Listen friend, is not a magic it is real, very real that can be proof by you. God does not leave himself without a proof.

Please also understand that God is everywhere, He is not a respecter of persons or places, so he is with you where ever you are so recognize him and he will proof himself for you in the area that concerns you. Proof him today and remain ever bless.

Bible said in

philipians4 v13

I can do all things through Christ who strengthen me.

Is God many? The creator of heaven and earth, the maker of all things, the giver of life and every good thing on earth is one. The bible said in **exodus** that his name is Jehovah, I AM THAT I AM, He is the only true God and above Him, there is no one else. Please know that Jesus Christ is the begotten son of God and he (GOD) has Glorify his son Jesus Christ by giving a name that is above all names. Therefore he is the Lord of Glory. Jesus is Lord because in

phillipians2v9

Wherefore God also hath highly exalted him, and given him a name which is above every name.

And

John3v 16

For God so loved the world, that he gave his only begotten son, that whosoever believeth in him should not perish, but have everlasting life.

This means we must believe in him. Now true followers of Christ must love their neighbors as their selves irrespective of their religion, race and status because the bible said, love your neighbor as yourself and even in Islam, they teaches love. So bombing churches and mosque and market places are there love in that? It simply means that they are not true followers of Christ or ALLAH. If Jesus is one of the prophet of God, as they believe in Islam, has God [Allah] ever said that people should kill their neighbors rather than love? Why then are their much bombing in the northern Nigeria, Pakistan, Iraq and Afghanistan, Libya and Iran?

Recently, as a result of much bombing by Boko Hara in Nigeria, there was a visit by a Muslim brother to the president and he said that there is no teaching in Islam that encourage killing and also for my own curiosity have ask some Muslims if the five vigil story is true but they decline, So where is the killing in Nigeria coming from? The bombing of Churches, Mosques, and kidnapping of school girls. Nyanya motor park explosion where are they coming from? Are they political? Why will a leader wish to use violence to take power? Some Muslim brothers may not give their daughter to a Christian son and the Christian brothers will not want to give his daughter to a Muslim son why? Because they both feel that they are better than the other.

This book is not just for Christians alone but for everybody because identity crisis is affecting everybody. I pray that the spirit of love and selflessness be upon every life on earth in Jesus name Amen.

God is not divided so be not divided, for all are the children of the Most High God whether someone believe it or not. I beseech Christians and Muslims to know that irrespective of their belief that they still from one God which means they are one. Is quit unfortunate to kill with a belief that you are fighting for God because the God I know is too powerful for a man to fight for Him.

All of these troubles are upon the youths of today because through the youths the devil carries out all these evil and at the end, it cost some their lives, some employments, educations, marriages and movement and most importantly, it cost them eternal life. The Boko Haran and the Niger Delta militants are all youths and 90 percent of the lives loss in any blast are youths which is not what God require from man. But what does GOD require from man? God require love and peace from and to all men and also praises because the bible said in the book of

Exdus23v25-26

And ye shall serve the LORD thy God, and he shall bless thy bread, and thy water; and I will take sickness away from the midst of thee.

26: There shall nothing cast their young, nor be barren, in thy land: the number of thy days I will fulfill.

Therefore serve the Lord He take sickness and barrenness away from you and bless your bread and water then will you be bless. Also when you obey his word you will surely prosper. This is also the deliverance of all, serving the LORD God.

job36v11;

If they obey and serve him, they shall spend their days in prosperity, and their years in pleasure.

Therefore bless his holy name and he will satisfy you with good things. He will also redeem you from destructions. ALL MANNERS OF TROUBLES, like heart diseases, brain tumor, diabetics AandB

Psalms103v1-5

Bless the LORD, O my soul: and all that is within me, bless his holy name.

2 Bless the LORD, O my soul, and forget not all his benefits:

3: Who forgiveth all thine iniquities; who healeth all thy diseases;

4 Who redeemeth thy life from destruction; who crowneth thee with lovingkindness and tender mercies;

5 Who satisfieth thy mouth with good things; so that thy youth is renewed like the eagle's.

Magnify him and he will protect you, keep you and also lead you

Isaiah45V2-5.

2: I will go before thee, and make the crooked places straight: I will break in pieces the gates of brass, and cut in sunder the bars of iron:

3: And I will give thee the treasures of darkness, and hidden riches of secret place, that thou mayest know that I the LORD, which called by thy name, am the God of Israel.

4: For Jacob my servant's sake, and Israel mine elect, I have even called thee by thy name: I have surnamed thee, though thou hast not known me:

5: I am the LORD, and there is none else, there is no God beside me: I girded thee, though thou hast not known me:

Recognize him as the only source and he will teach you to profits, in health, education, family life and much more.

Isaiah48v17

Thus saith the LORD, thy redeemer, the Holy one of Israel; I am the LORD thy God which teachest thee to profit, which leadeth thee by the way that thou shouldest go

Also know that our LORD God is a jealous God

Exodus20v5

Thou shall not bow down thy self to them, nor serve them: for I the LORD thy God am a jealous God,......

Please understand that our God is not an alternative God so if you want him in your life, then let him be your only way.

Remember him in all you do, that is putting him first in your life and he will make you rich **Deuteronomy 8v18**

But thou shall remember the LORD thy God: for it he that giveth thee power to get wealth, that he may establish his covenant which he sware unto thy fathers, as it is this day.

and open the windows of heaven and pour out his blessings

Malachi3v10

...saith the LORD of hosts. If I will not open you the windows of heaven, and pour you out a blessing, that there shall not be room enough to receive it.

Because God changeth not, God will rebuke the devourer for your sake. Please understand that sicknesses are devourers, troubles of all kinds are devourers, whatever that is not in the life of Jesus is a devourer. So by remembering Him in all these, He will surely fight for you

Exodus14V14

The LORD shall fight for you, and ye shall hold your peace.

God will also take away sickness and bless your bread and water you will never see them again

Exodus 15v26

.... I will put none of these diseases upon thee, which I have brought upon the Egyptians: for I am the LORD that healeth thee.

Christians should note that a house that is divided cannot stand. Therefore denomination should not be a problem in the house of God. In the book of

1cor3v3-23.

3:For ye are yet carnal: for whereas there is among you envying, and strife, and divisions, are ye not yet carnal, and walk as men?

4 For while one saith, I am of Paul; and another, I am of Apollos; are ye not carnal?

5 Who then is Paul, and who is Apollos, but ministers by whom ye believed, even as the Lord gave to every man?

6 I have planted, Apollos watered; but God gave the increase.

7 So then neither is he that planted anything, neither he that watereth; but God that giveth the increase.

8:Now he that planted and he that watereth are one: and every man shall receive his own reward according to his labour.

9:.. For we are labourers together with God: ye are God's husbandry, ye are Gods building.

So why are these questions? I am redeem, I am a winner, I am a deeper life, am catholic, no I can't go to that program because is not my

Church. Listen friends don't go to that church because girls are putting on trouser. No I cannot go to that church because they preach only prosperity, do you see that church/ Holy Spirit is not there. See! Don't believe on that miracle because there is no such thing as miracle because it ended after that Jesus ascends to heaven. I like my church but I don't like yours, my church is good, my church is better, my church is best. I like my pastor, no I don't like him, I like the way my pastor speaks; no I don't like him because he makes himself a god. Did you hear what that priest did? Therefore they are not godly.

These are what have been happening in Christianity. Now according to the bible "is these not envies, strife and even division? Do we not worship one God through Jesus Christ? Will your church stand on your behalf in the day of judgments? Is salvation not personal? Why then will somebody bring down instead of building the house of God? That's why there is much problem in the church today because of identity crisis. I pray that every divisions among churches be destroy in Jesus name Amen.

2cor5v10.

For we must all appear before the judgment seat of Christ; that every one may receive the things done in his body, according to that he hath done, whether it be good or bad.

Finally brethren, understand that the only source of victory is Christ Jesus. He teaches us to love one another because He alone is the way the truth and the life and no one goes to the father but through him. And loving one another means that whether pagan or Christian or Muslim must love each other as their selves.

If love comes into us the problem of misunderstanding will be solve because the bible said that love covereth all things. Therefore let us give love a chance.

Misunderstanding is a product of identity crisis because MR A said my own is the best and MR B said no my own is the best. If this identity crisis is solved, there will be fewer troubles on earth. Troubles like wars, divorce rate, and every other thing that have in one way or the other trouble people. I pray that everyone that comes across this book be richly and supernaturally bless in Jesus name Amen.

Chapter 2

FEAR

The earth is shaken, deaths are rising, disasters everywhere and hatred, Terrorism and bribe.

The world is changing with speed, injustice and wickedness all along.

Pains, regret and sorrows dwell among men. But the darkness shall cover the earth, and gross darkness the people: but the LORD shall arise upon thee, and his glory shall be seen upon thee.

Deadly diseases even with the amazing medical equipments but yea though I walk through the valley of the shadow of death, I will fear no evil: for thou art with me.

It is obvious that the earth has experience great evil but there is a sure way of victory for the children of God. "For he that is in us is greater than he that is in the world" though we be in the world, but not of the world. Therefore, things happen for a reason and most importantly for the good of the children of God.

1thessalonians5v18:

In everything give thanks: for this is the will of God in Christ Jesus concerning you.

Now, no matter the happenings on earth, the earth is still on motion. But what is God saying concerning all of these?

''Behold, I will do a new thing: now it shall spring forth; shall ye not know it? I will even make a way in the wilderness, and rivers in the desert. ''

So this brings us to the second topic of this book. I want to affirm that through the grace of God in my life, that every Word of God in this book is true and it subject to personal experience. Understand that what ever seen impossible to you in this book, God has made it possible through Jesus Christ his dear son. And anything that looks foolish to you don't boarder your brain with it just go on.

Fear generally means a feelings of insecurity, feelings of pending danger. Fear in other hand, makes someone not to act as he intended to because it paralyze the faculty of imagination, visions and insight, and at times kills self reliance. It promote procrastination; thinking that things will get better as the time elapses, but the reverse turn out to be the case, when fear is not subdued.

Fear make's self control difficult if not impossible. It destroys the possibilities of accurate thinking, it diverts power into nothingness. Fear destroys ambitions, blurred memory and invites failures of different forms. Fear make's love difficult because it devours the emotions of the heart which discourage friendship both with God and man.

Fear is one of the battles the youths are facing today because it invites disaster into some lives which leads to sleeplessness, misery, sadness and so many other similar vices. But what is God saying concerning this word fear? In the book of

Isaiah41v10-13:

Fear thou not; for I am with thee: be not dismayed; for I am thy God: I will strengthen thee; yea, I will help thee; yea, I will uphold thee with the right hand of my righteousness.

11: Behold, all they that were incense against thee shall be ashamed and confounded: they shall be as nothing; and they that strife with thee shall perish.

12: Thou shall seek them, and shalt not find them, even them that contended with thee: they that war against thee shall be as nothing, and as a thing of nought.

13: For I the LORD thy God will hold thy right hand, saying unto thee, Fear not; I will help thee.

Therefore, in this subject, we shall be dealing with the two kinds of fears, the advantages and the disadvantages. And at the end we will know the solution to it

1) **Fear of the natural man.**
2) **Fear of the supernatural man.**

Fear of the natural man.

I used the word "natural man" to classify a person whom has not yet known or believed the power of our Lord Jesus Christ, according to the book of

1cor2v14:

But the natural man receiveth not the things of the spirit of God: for they are foolishness unto him: neither can he know them, because they are spiritually discerned.

Now, if there is a natural man, then there is a supernatural man. But it is sad that billions of youths today are still in the level of a natural man. So in the natural man, we shall be looking on what are the curses of fear and the solutions and also for the supernatural man.

Now these are some of the curses of fear of the natural man.

1: Poverty.

2: Over caution.

3: Procrastination.

4: Sickness.

5: Fear of the unknown.

Poverty: the natural man is afraid of poverty because he too wants to be known and have many friends as the bible said

proverb14v20:

The poor is hated even of his own neighbor: but the rich hath many friends.

Therefore the natural man does a lot of things whether good or evil just to get away from the fear of lack or wants, poverty. But, why the fear? Because he know not his God. For it is written, for they that do know their God will do exploit. Why the fear of poverty?because they remember Him not, the owner of everything on earth and heaven. The bible said in

Deutronomy8v18:

But thou shalt remember the LORD thy God for it is he that giveth thee power to get wealth; that he may establish his covenant which he swore unto thy fathers as it is this day.

God has already sworn to bless us but why are we not seeing it? Why are we not seeing the blessings of the lord in our lives? Because the owner of heaven and earth is not recognize in our life.

Psalms24v1:

The earth is the LORD's and the fullness thereof the world and they that dwell therein.

Please note, that the wish of God towards us is prosperity according to His Word in

3John2

Beloved I WISH ABOVE ALL THINGS THAT THOU MAYEST PROSPER AND BE IN HEALTH EVEN AS THY SOUL PROSPERETH

Meaning that we are permitted to prosper. Even our soul will also prosper. That is our portion in the LORD. The bible said in

Job22v21-26:

21: Acquaint now thyself with him and be at peace: thereby good shall come unto thee.

22: Receive, I pray thee, the law from his mouth, and lay up his words in thine heart.

V23: if thou return to the almighty, thou shall be build up,thou shall put away iniquity far from thy tabernacle.

24: Then shall thou lay up gold as dust and the gold of ophir as the stones of the brooks.

25: Yea, the almighty God shall be thy defence and thou shalt have plenty of silver.

26: For then shall thy have thy delight in the Almighty, and shall lift up thy face unto God.

Therefore meet with Jesus Christ and be at peace thereby shall good come unto. Also in

Matthew 6v25-33

Therefore I say unto you, take no thought for your life,what we shall eat,or what ye shall drink ;nor yet for your body,what ye shall put on .Is not the life more than meat,and the body than raiment?

26: Behold the fowls of the air; they sow not, neither do they reap,nor gather into barns; yet your heavenly father feedeth them. Are ye not much better than they?

30: Wherefore, if God clothe the grass of the field, which today is, and tomorrow is cast into oven, shall He not much more clothe you, O ye of little faith?

33: But seek ye first the kingdom of God, and his righteousness; and all these things shall be added unto you

Isaiah49v13-16:

Sing, O heaven: and be joyful o earth; and break forth into singings, O mountains; for the LORD has comforted his people, and will have mercy upon his afflicted

14: But Zion said, the LORD hath forsaken me and my LORD hath forgotten me.

15: Can a woman forget her sucking child, that she should not have compassion on the son of her womb? Yea, they may forget, yet will I not forget thee

16: Behold, I have graven thee upon the palms of hands; thy walls are continually before me.

So before we ask, God already knows. You see, He will never forget us because our walls are continually before Him. So my friend, seek the LORD first and Poverty will never know your address in life. Poverty as we know, is an evil disease, therefore is a bad place to be, you know why? Because I have been there and will never want anybody to be close to it.

Please understand that when a man is without money and unable to get a job, something happens to him that can be observe by the people around him; as his shoulder, his movement and even his countenance will begin to sag. He cannot escape the feeling of inferiority complex in the midst of people with money and good employment even when he knows that they are not his equals in character, intelligence or abilities.

Do you want to feel inferior or unfortunate? If your answer is No! Which must, and then accept Jesus Christ as your Lord and personal savior because He is the only way? It might be grievous, but he is the only hope. So seek him now that he may be found and all other things will be added to you

Deutro28v1-8:

And it shall come to pass, if thou shall hearken diligently unto the voice of the LORD thy God, to observe and to do all his commandments which I command thee this day, that the LORD thy God will set thee on high above all nations of the earth.

2: And all these blessings shall come on thee, and over take thee if thou shalt hearken unto the voice of the LORD thy God.

3: Blessed shalt thou be in the city and blessed shalt thou be in the field.

4: Blessed shall be the fruit of thy body, and the fruit of thy ground, and the fruit of thy cattle, the increase of thy kine, and the flocks of thy sheep.

5: Blessed shall be thy basket and thy store.

6: Blessed shalt thou be when thou comest in, and blessed shalt thou be when thou goest out.

7: The LORD shall cause thine enemies that rise up against thee to be smitten before thy face: they shall come out against thee one way, and flee before thee seven ways.

8: The LORD shall command the blessing upon thee in thy storehouses, and in all that thou settest thine hand

unto; and he shall bless thee in the land which the LORD thy God giveth thee.

In everything God does for humans, there is always a part the person must play. "Do this and I will do that" that is it.

Deut.28v1

....to observe and to do all his commandments which I command thee this day,

You see, to observe and to do all his commandments. That is what to do to receive the desires of our hearts.

According to the bible that said wisdom is profitable to direct I want to highlight some causes of poverty

1. **Over cautious:** fear of poverty brings the spirit of over cautiousness. Please understand that people with this spirit have the habit of looking for the negative side of everything, why? Because the true spirit of God is not upon them because God is positive. This spirit of over cautiousness makes them thinks and talks about possible failure instead of concentrating on the means of succeeding. Over cautiousness brings people or their victims to the road of disaster but never search for a way to avoid failure. The fear of poverty makes people only remember the people that failed and forgets those who succeeded because they are afraid to start and finally dwell on past mistakes without making any effort to improve.

2. **Procrastinations:** this is also a great enemy of success and the biggest promoter of poverty. This is the habit of patting off until tomorrow that which should be done today maybe because of the fear of precious failures or fear of failing. It is commonly expressed through lack of strong will power, willingness to tolerate poverty, acceptance of whatever life offer without protest, lack of enthusiasm, mental and physical laziness.

   Please understand that if you want to succeed in life you must reject this illness called procrastination because it has rendered many great dreams, ideas and visions unrealized; therefore be very careful about the illness called procrastination because it is a silent killer the act of waiting for tomorrow. Therefore start now to kill it by having to do list. Outlined by their importance. I pray that the grace and strength to accomplish your plans, visions, ambitions be given to you in the name of Jesus Amen

3. **Sickness:** Sickness is a curse! The natural man is always afraid. The natural man is always in danger. Why? Because if we are not in Christ we are in crisis. Many believe in several things, some say there is God another said there is no God. and some trust in Doctors, some in God, but I have seen whom the doctor gave 1 hour to live and I prayed a short prayer and she lived unto this day, I have seen a verdict of a doctor of HIV /AIDS positive becomes negative I have seen SS becoming AA gen, dead comes back to life. Mine self was given 6 months to live in 2002. I have seen with my eyes many undeniable miracles including a cripple walking but in all of these I have never seen or heard that God said something and it did not come to pass. Now with the little experience of my life with God, will I ever believe the Doctors verdicts? Or believed that, there is any sickness called incurable? in the books of

Luke1
37: For with God nothing shall be impossible.
45: And blessed is she that believed: for there shall be performance of those things which were told her from the Lord.
Also the bible said that the kingdom of God is not words alone but in power
1Corinthians4v20.
For the kingdom of God is not in word, but in power.
To me all things are possible because GOD said so and his Word is final. God had said that all the impossible sickness of man is possible to him. Therefore, I said no sickness is incurable because if it is impossible for Doctors, is not impossible for God. So there shall be nothing as **a right to die** because the knowledge or wisdom of man fails.

please note, I am not saying that Doctors or medical treatment is wrong because it was God that gave the wisdom to create the equipment and all that is used in hospitals, I am not saying

that physicians don't know what they are really doing but am bringing the power of God upon us, not to accept that word **no way** because the good news here is that there are ways. **psalms24v1. The earth is in the LORD's, and the fullness thereof; the world and they that dwell therein.**
God does not lack ways! Never! Therefore I beseech everyone to seek God first in any situation of these words

   a. **Right to die**
   b. **You have this day to live**
   c. **There is no cure**
   d. **You are not going to make it.**

Please refuse it and seek God immediately whether you or your relatives, friends or anybody you know. Go to any man of God ask him to pray with you or if I can be reached, reach me.

Natural man fears sickness because of the ugly and terrible pictures which have been painted in his mind of what may happen if sickness strikes. Sometimes, it may be the fear of finance which the sickness may claim.

The seed of fear of sickness dwells in every minds of the natural man as a matter of fact but nobody desired to be ill

Jeremiah8v22,

Is there no balm in Gilead; is there no physician there? Why then is not the health of the daughter of my people recovered?

The reason why the health is not recovered is because they don't know who the healer was. Medical practitioners know this truth that they treat but God heals.

As I said earlier, if we are not in Christ we are in Crisis because only those in Christ knows who the healer is, and if you don't know him, He is Jesus Christ.

Mark.16v15-18;

15: And he said unto them, go ye into all the world, and preach the gospel to every creature.

16" He that believeth and is baptized shall be saved; but he that believeth not shall be damned.

17: And these signs shall follow them that believe; in my name shall they cast out devils; they shall speak with new tongues;

18" They shall take up serpents; and if they drink any deadly thing, it not hurt them, they shall lay hands on the sick, and they shall recover.

You will have the power as soon you know him and believe that he is your Lord and personal savior, Millions of people has loss their lives because of Lack of this Knowledge.

Proverb.11v14

Where no counsel is, the people fall; but in the multitude of counselors there is safety.

So this is the safety, Jesus is able to do all things.

Eph3v20

Now unto him that is able to do exceeding abundantly above all that we ask or think, according to the power that worketh in us.

so there is power that worketh in us but it must be activated by acknowledging God as the only way, Please remember that for God to do anything for you, you must do something too, so here are some to do because they are the same curses of sickness today in the lives of the Youths.

1. **Hypochondria**

2. Drug Abuse

Hypochondria: This is a state in which people worry over their health. They believe that they are sick whereas there is nothing of such. So we must avoid worrying over our health because the Bible says in the book of

Isaiah.53v4-5

Surely he hath borne our grieves, and carried our sorrows yet we did esteem him stricken, smitten of God,and afflicted.

5:But he was wounded for our transgressions, he was bruised

Therefore people should know that they are already healed by His (Jesus) stripes. All they have to do is believe. Remember in the Bible the story of Naaman when he was asked by Prophet Elijah to go down to River Jordan and dip himself seven (7) times. It was like a joke to him but when he gave it a try, His body was restored. The Bible says Fear not therefore fear not. In

Isaiah41 v10-14.

Fear thou not; for I am with thee: be not dismayed; for I am thy God: I will strengthen thee; yea, I will help thee; yea, I will uphold thee with the right hand of my righteousness.

11: Behold, all they that were incensed against thee shall be ashamed and confounded: they shall be as nothing; and they that strive with thee shall perish.

12: Thou shalt seek them, and shalt not find them, even them that contended with thee: they that war against thee shall be as nothing, and as a thing of nought.

13: For I the LORD thy God will hold thy right hand, saying unto thee, Fear not; I will help thee.

14: Fear not, thou worm Jacob, and ye men of Israel; I will help thee, saith the LORD, and thy redeemer, the Holy One of Israel.

1. **Drug Abuse:** I met someone smoking and drinking and I ask him, what pleasures do you derived from this? But his responds was that he wants to forget his problems. Then I ask why? And he said; whenever I drink and smoke likes this, I go home and sleep without thinking. I met a young girl smoking and I ask. "You like it? She said is not like I like it but I can't eat unless I smoke. I met someone, a smoker and I ask her what can I do for you to quit smoking and her reply was that if she did not drink or smoke in the morning, it will be as if something is taken out from her.

   Some people actually resort to the use of alcohol, narcotics or other drugs just to minimize or destroy a mild pain that can subside on its own. Avoid the use of certain drugs you know cannot do anything good in you. Drug Abuse has recorded several death cases resulting by excess and continual abuse of drugs, there is nothing that can take away pains than God. Therefore meet with him now.

   FEAR OF LOSS OF LOVE: The word love originated from God and he also instructed us to love our neighbors as our selves.

John 3-16

For God so loved the world, that he gave his only begotten Son, that whosoever believeth in him should not perish, but have everlasting life.

God never said in anywhere that we should be afraid of love. Though it is in the nature of man to love and wish to be loved and cherished. It is also in his nature to think of the possibility of losing the love and affection of a beloved. But this is not the will of God concerning love upon man but because of the right of choice or rather the free will to choose given by God to man, some choose to be ordinary while some choose to be like God.

Deutr30:15-16

15: **See, I have set before thee this day life and good, and death and evil;**

16: **In that I command thee this day to love the LORD thy God, to walk in his ways, and to keep his commandments and his statutes and his judgments, that thou mayest live and multiply: and the LORD thy God shall bless thee in the land whither thou goest to possess it. .**

The natural man is a fearful man because he doesn't know how to possess his possessions in the kingdom of God. The fear of losing some loved ones has caused several pains and some time death in the life of youths. The fear of losing a loved one with time will bring jealousy and other similar neurosis.

When I was in secondary school, I had a girlfriend that I loved so much that I believed I could do anything for her, just to keep her around, one day she had a financial problem that I could not solve and she knew that I did not have that amount of money but that her problem needed a solution. so I went to my parents and lied about something that will make them give me money, but I still could not get all the money she needed, finally she said to me that she could not go out with someone who could not afford her bills. Five weeks later I discovered that she actually left me because she had been going out with a boy that was financially buoyant. Now if I had steal or engaged in other related vices just to provide the money or other valuables for the loved one; thinking that love can be bought because of the fear of losing the love of their heart. And if I had produced that money, wouldn't she dump me after all?

Because of this natural fear of losing loved ones, some people incurred depts. in order to make their loved ones financially comfortable. But it is not what God wants because love is a free gift from God. So it cannot be purchased anywhere in the market. Please note that money is also a part of love because without it life can be boring but do not engage in evil so as to make money to impress a loved one because every man shall appear before God in judgment personally not you and your loved one because you are all alone

Eccl. 12v13-14,

Let us hear the conclusion of the whole matter: Fear God, and keep his commandments: for this is the whole duty of man.

14: For God shall bring every work into judgment, with every secret thing, whether it be good, or whether it be evil.

2 Corinth 5:10

For we must all appear before the judgment seat of Christ; that every one may receive the things done in his body, according to that he hath done, whether it be good or bad.

Several times youths steal not because they want to steal but because they want to satisfy a loved one, therefore I pray that every spirit of fear be removed in Jesus Name Amen. Please remember, the solution to all of these fears is Jesus Christ. He is the only way, therefore go to him and have rest from all oppressions of the devils

Isaiah 54: 14

In righteousness shalt thou be established: thou shalt be far from oppression; for thou shalt not fear: and from terror; for it shall not come near thee.

THE FEAR OF THE UNKNOWN: I realize that many people are afraid of their future, afraid of their lives especially with the look of things in this world. Sometimes people are afraid but cannot explain the source or the cause of it. In Japan after the Tsunami much people were afraid of what happened then and are afraid of what might happen in the future. The earth has recorded a lot of earth quake, tsunami's, hurricane, road accident, loss of air craft, ship sinking and explosions of all kinds, wars, kidnapping, robbery and assassination of various levels and some people are also manipulated by demons and other complaints of seeing strange faces that cannot be identified by others, others said they heard strange voices. But in all of these, what did God ask us to do? fear not, say God because he knew all of these will come that is what is said in the book of

Isaiah 41: 10 – 14

10: **Fear thou not; for I am with thee: be not dismayed; for I am thy God: I will strengthen thee; yea, I will help thee; yea, I will uphold thee with the right hand of my righteousness.**

11: **Behold, all they that were incensed against thee shall be ashamed and confounded: they shall be as nothing; and they that strive with thee shall perish.**

12: **Thou shalt seek them, and shalt not find them, even them that contended with thee: they that war against thee shall be as nothing, and as a thing of nought.**

13: **For I the LORD thy God will hold thy right hand, saying unto thee,**

14 **Fear not; I will help thee. Fear not, thou worm Jacob, and ye men of Israel; I will help thee, saith the LORD, and thy redeemer, the Holy One of Israel.**

Isaiah 43: 1 -4

*1:***But now thus saith the LORD that created thee, O Jacob, and he that formed thee, O Israel, Fear not: for I have redeemed thee, I have called thee by thy name; thou art mine.**

2: When thou passest through the waters, I will be with thee; and through the rivers, they shall not overflow thee: when thou walkest through the fire, thou shalt not be burned; neither shall the flame kindle upon thee.

3: For I am the LORD thy God, the Holy One of Israel, thy Saviour: I gave Egypt for thy ransom, Ethiopia and Seba for thee.

4: Fear not: for I am with thee: I will bring thy seed from the east, and gather thee from the west;

He that is not in Christ is in crisis and I cannot allow us to be ignorant of it. Therefore accept Christ and be at peace. A peaceful person doesn't worry about tomorrow because he knows who he is. David knew who he is that is why in

psalms 23:4: **Yea, though I walk through the valley of the shadow of death, I will fear no evil: for thou art with me; thy rod and thy staff they comfort me.**

Don't fear my friends only rejoice in the LORD thy God the maker of heaven and earth. In God there is peace.

Job 22:21. **Acquaint now thyself with him, and be at peace: thereby good shall come unto thee.**

Receive peace that will subdue every form of fear in your life in Jesus Name Amen. The fear of the unknown is largely in Africa because of the low rate of development, some now believe that going to Europe or America or Asia will be the short cut to fulfilling their dreams of becoming rich. But this is only a wish that things will get better as soon as they find their way to Europe and wishes that is not from God is subjected to change and when that happens, they regret ever leaving their home town why? Because they are afraid of the unknown, the future.

I want you to understand that, is only the devil that has the spirit of fear, the Bible says for I have not given you the spirit of fear but of power and love and of a sound mind. God has finished his work on every living creature though some don't know his work upon them but you can know by asking him in prayers

> *Phillip 4:6 – 7*Be careful for nothing; but in everything by prayer and supplication with thanksgiving let your requests be made known unto God.

> 7 And the peace of God, which passeth all understanding, shall keep your hearts and minds through Christ Jesus.

God is everywhere so there is no special place to pray therefore start praying now as to obtain grace of God that will lift you above all forms of fears and worries. I pray that the grace of God abide in your life in Jesus name Amen.

Fear of the supernatural man

This is used to classify the believers, someone that belief in the powers of Jesus Christ. "That Jesus Christ is Lord" and he is the only way to salvation.

This book is not basically for believers alone because I believe that every believer should know the authority of the believer which the LORD gave through His dear son Jesus Christ. So I believe that a true believer must know his or her right in the kingdom of God. Because according to the book of

1cori4v20 For the kingdom of God is not in word, but in power. and what is power? We all know that power makes things or people do as you want without objection or options. Thus, every man in Christ has this power to dominate his territory no matter the challenges.

> *Luke 10v19*

> Behold, I give unto you power to tread on serpents and scorpions, and over all the power of the enemy: and nothing shall by any means hurt you.

Mark 16: 15-18,

And he said unto them, Go ye into all the world, and preach the gospel to every creature.

16: He that believeth and is baptized shall be saved; but he that believeth not shall be damned.

17: And these signs shall follow them that believe; In my name shall they cast out devils; they shall speak with new tongues;

18They shall take up serpents; and if they drink any deadly thing, it shall not hurt them; they shall lay hands on the sick, and they shall recover.

These are the exploit of the true believer of Christ so I believe that all believers are doing exploits because it is written that they that do know their God will do exploits.

But what is the requirement for all these exploits because in everything there are requirements. For example for someone to travel to another country he must have either a passport or an identity card then if visa is required he must have it for him to be able to travel to the country of his choice. So is Christianity, you must be Identified first by giving your life to Christ and then you will be permitted to explore the goodness of the Lord.

Now concerning the fear of the supernatural man is THE FEAR OF THE LORD. As a citizen of a country, you are expected to respect the rules and regulations of the country not only the citizens alone but also everyone that lives and works in that country. So keeping the laws of the nation is applicable to the fear of the LORD in Christendom. Bible says so in

proverbs 9:10.

The fear of the LORD is the beginning of wisdom: and the knowledge of the holy is understanding.

So wisdom is in the fear of the LORD. The reason being that when you fear the LORD, you obtain mercies and grace to do the impossible but if you refuse you run dry, and no true believer WILL WANT TO RUN DRY. Because God is the only source of his survival so he must attach himself to his sources.

Please note, any Lake that does not link to a river will certainly or suddenly gets dry one day because there will be no supply in dry seasons. Therefore believers must link themselves with God because the supplier of all their needs is from him, and there is only one way to get it, and that is THE FEAR OF THE LORD (knowing the right thing to do and doing it). Also my friend I beseech thee to give your life to Christ now by saying this prayer "Lord Jesus I come to you as a sinner, I ask for your mercies and compassion, I ask of your forgiveness for all my sins. I believe you died to save me and rose on the third day. Thank you for saving me, now I'm a born again. That is it, welcome to the kingdom of God where nothing is impossible, and enjoy your flight to heaven where you belong.

Therefore I pray for you today, everything that has not been working in your life, start working now in Jesus name, in every evil situation you find yourself be out now in Jesus name, every sickness that has trouble you be healed now in Jesus name, every spirit of confusion in your life be destroyed in Jesus name Amen, you are blessed in Jesus name Amen.

I encourage you to get a bible if you don't have any and always pray, am sure that you must testify the presence of God in your life from this day forward.

When God wants to change people's locations, he changes their allocation, not location before allocation. Understanding the Word of God about Health shows that health is wealth. No matter how rich someone might be without a healthy life that same person is poor. Because the woman with the issue of blood spent all she had yet no solution was found. so an ill health can sweep all that someone had. Please understand that nothing can stop sickness on earth except Jesus Christ. Presidents, governors, senators, doctors and all other works of life have died of it. People who are physically rich and spiritually poor have died of it. Now being physically rich does not make someone rich and being physically poor does not make one poor but understanding the purpose of God concerning your life is what makes you what you are, and that your name is written in heavens book of life *luke 10:17-20*

And the seventy returned again with joy, saying, Lord, even the devils are subject unto us through thy name.

18 And he said unto them, I beheld Satan as lightning fall from heaven.

19Behold, I give unto you power to tread on serpents and scorpions, and over all the power of the enemy: and nothing shall by any means hurt you.

20 Notwithstanding in this rejoice not, that the spirits are subject unto you; but rather rejoice, because your names are written in heaven.

Therefore, no matter how rich someone might be without Christ, the person only exists not surviving. Because it's impossible to survive in a foreign land without acknowledging the rules and regulation that governs that land. Therefore remember the earth is the Lord's

psalm 24:1.

The earth is the LORD's, and the fulness thereof; the world, and they that dwell therein.

No matter how rich someone might be without Christ, without heaven, it's a perpetual disease because he has consciously laid up riches for stranger even with pains. Understand that healing starts by believing, that is having the knowledge that whatever the sickness may be, it is possible to overcome it with Jesus Christ but the believer don't get healed because they are on divine Health already. Thus sickness is for unbelievers! Begging is also against the purpose of God concerning its children. If we understand the purpose of God, we will know that lack or begging is an insult to redemption because we are fashioned to be at the top

Deuteronomy28:12 – 13.

The LORD shall open unto thee his good treasure, the heaven to give the rain unto thy land in his season, and to bless all the work of thine hand: and thou shalt lend unto many nations, and thou shalt not borrow.

13: And the LORD shall make thee the head, and not the tail; and thou shalt be above only, and thou shalt not be beneath; if that thou hearken unto the commandments of the LORD thy God, which I command thee this day, to observe and to do them:

Healing is not a wish, but it is labored for. Because without believe, there is no healing.

Luke I: 45

And blessed is she that believed: for there shall be a performance of those things which were told her from the Lord.

Also understand that not everyone that shouts for healing actually wants to be healed. And understand that the fact that someone went to a pastor for healing is never a guarantee that he or she will be heal. And if he is rich and think that God will be fast to heal him because pastors goes to his house to pray, without humbling his heart to God, no healing will come to such person because God cannot be bought with money. Some accept Jesus as savior but not as Lord. I know this because many are still suffering even in the house of God where Holy Angels administer to people. They go to church yet nothing to show for it, no sign of repentance or proof that they are in the kingdom of God. Why? Because Satan still torments them day and night; a lot of evils happen to this group of people that believe in Jesus as their savior but not as their Lord. They claim they serve and believe God but they don't, this is what I call sheep in wolf clothing.

Christianity is not magic, God blesses by the works of his people's hands *psalms1:3* **And he shall be like a tree planted by the rivers of water, that bringeth forth his fruit in his season; his leaf also shall not wither; and whatsoever he doeth shall prosper.**

What will God prosper in your hands? What do you want? Healing? Baby? Miracles? Durable Marriage? Jobs and other needs, God can do it all but there is a price for it, and if you are willing to pay it, you will have all that you desire, whether it is possible to man or not. Acknowledging God is the price to pay for us to have it all. Remembers He is able.

eph 3:20. **Now unto him that is able to do exceeding abundantly above all that we ask or think, according to the power that worketh in us,**

Therefore praise him for all he has done for you and also in anticipation of what you want him to do for you. Praise is the plural of prayer because praises does twice as nice. Accept Jesus Christ today and be at peace

Also if you believe that you can prosper in your country within a short time, you see it coming to pass because our thoughts will make it works in us and according to the Bible.

PROVERBS 23: 7

For as he thinketh in his heart, so is he:

So if as a man thinketh in his heart so is he; it means that what we think is us. Therefore start thinking right, think positively and receive positive things.

If the Americans believed in going outside their country to work, I don't think people especially youths of today will risk their lives just to go there.

Demons have possessed people by making them idolize places, making them believe that without there, there is no way else, in so doing, creating enmity between them and their God. People leave the ultimate in search of alternative. I pray that whatever the devil has done to anyone in this regards be destroyed in Jesus name Amen and anything humiliating till date must give way in Jesus mighty name Amen, Isaac sow in the land and reap hundred fold that same year in the same place that was in famine, and the philistine envied him.

GEN 26:12-14

Then Isaac sowed in that land, and received in the same year an hundredfold: and the LORD blessed him.

13: And the man waxed great, and went forward, and grew until he became very great:

14: For he had possession of flocks, and possession of herds, and great store of servants: and the Philistines envied him.

This is certainly a battle that we must win and we cannot win it alone; so allow God to help you. He is your only hope of victory. Where was our father Abraham when the LORD called him? Today Abraham is the father of nations. Through him the earth was blessed but he was 75 years old when he answered the calling of God and that change everything about him. So it does not matter your age or where you are, only obey the Words of God because His thoughts are higher than yours.

GEN 12:1-3

Now the LORD had said unto Abram, Get thee out of thy country, and from thy kindred, and from thy father's house, unto a land that I will shew thee:

2: And I will make of thee a great nation, and I will bless thee, and make thy name great; and thou shalt be a blessing:

3: And I will bless them that bless thee, and curse him that curseth thee: and in thee shall all families of the earth be blessed.

JEREMIAH 29:11-12

For I know the thoughts that I think toward you, saith the LORD, thoughts of peace, and not of evil, to give you an expected end.

12: Then shall ye call upon me, and ye shall go and pray unto me, and I will hearken unto you.

It doesn't matter the levels of your mistakes in life, pains and struggles. Abrahams was made a celebrity, a perpetual celebrity because he obeyed God and trust in Him. Therefore accept the calling of God in your life and be saved from the destruction of wrong thoughts and deeds.

Unbelief: Unbelief is the origin of all the problems the youths face on earth. Were a girl commits suicide just because her boy friend broke her heart or quit relationship. Sometimes the boy kill himself because of a relationship that he wasn't sure whether it will lead to marriage or not and if it will lead to marriage, did he not see the rate of divorce in recent years? So why will a promising young men or woman waste the potentials of God for the lust of the flesh and foolishness of the heart? Like I said before, there is no right for anyone to kill himself, or a right to die. Therefore, there is no right for anyone to kill himself or kill someone because of believe of any kind because Jesus Christ h*as* paid the price in full. Some might say" let kill him or her because her sickness is incurable and it will bring more pains to her and even to her family. See! It is good he die because he is suffering and not only him we also". But understand that what man cannot do God can. These things happen because man does not remember the original purpose of his creation and his duties on earth. If man recognize his status as a god, and know *his* abilities according to

GEN1:26-28

26: And God said, Let us make man in our image, after our likeness: and let them have dominion over the fish of the sea, and over the fowl of the air, and over the cattle,

and over all the earth, and over every creeping thing that creepeth upon the earth.

27: So God created man in his own image, in the image of God created he him; male and female created he them.

28: And God blessed them, and God said unto them, Be fruitful, and multiply, and replenish the earth, and subdue it: and have dominion over the fish of the sea, and over the fowl of the air, and over every living thing that moveth upon the earth.

Then man will never dream of killing himself because of diseases or pains. Understand that the dominion here involves. Sickness, anger, pride, witches $ wizards and poverty, also everything that is on the surface of the earth whether spiritual or physical. Therefore understand who you really are in the kingdom of God. Some girls or boys go as far as killing someone because of boy or girl friend in their lives. Now if this man or woman you kill for is gold he shouldn't have left you for another. Friendship is friendship; marriage is marriage none deserves to kill or kill for.

I have seen some trouble from similar things. In fact some years back. Someone slaps me because of his girl friend. Yet he couldn't stop boys from going to the girl. Even the girl loves the company of boys. today they are differently married. So if I had killed him for slapping me will he live today? But the girl will live, still marry another man. There is nothing that deserve the live of anybody because with all the medical equipment, surgeons, sorceries, medical experts, researchers including herbalist and Satan himself has never create a living being. Cars can be burnt; building destroyed, money loss and any other thing they can be gotten back because they are all manmade but not life. Life is from God. Therefore there is no right to die for someone or kill because you want to ease the pain of the victim family. Anger is what put us in trouble but pride is what keeps us there. I say this because some know the truth of something yet because of pride, they remain in the same thing. Forsake pride today and join the family of Christ and be at peace.

JOB 22:21

acquaint now thyself with him, and be at peace: thereby good shall come unto thee.

The acts of destroying things or house properties even injure themselves when angry is an act of ignorance and lack of self control. If they control themselves, they will realize that it is not the things they break or do to their flesh curse the pains or anger in them or will take away the anger.

They can kill the anger by been calm or is there a trophy in doing funny things such as that? When they make themselves bleed why go for treatment? They go because they can't stand the pains that come from it and also rearrange the house they scatter and buy whatever that was broken in the course of the action. Now the LORD God blessed us to be a blessing to others not to use the blessings or resources of God for fun or to oppress others in the society. God's wish for us is always good but our ways has been a hindrance to our blessing and at the end we sought for whom to blame. Come to God today and end all the miseries in your life. People think that worshiping God is doing God a favor. No, we worship God for who he is because he is the LORD of lords and King of kings. Imagine the respects that a presidents has in his country and around the world but God is the owner of heaven and earth yet people don't recognize him in *Daniel 4:29-37* even king Nebuchadnezzar been the ruler of other nations then was not rated equal with God, and finally he recognize God as the owner of everything on earth. And of course nothing is truly ours without Christ our lord.

If barrack Obama one day issue a paper that reads "my people of united state and the world in general I just realize that fornication is very bad therefore stop fornication. It will be pass as a law and many people will stop fornication because Barrack Obama say so but God that created all things including Obama had said from time in memorial that fornication is bad and many are not observing it. Now is man greater than God? God forbids, but people have idolized persons and believe whatever they say or do. Even doing what they do and has forsaken the original purpose of God in their lives: please note that Barrack Obama is used to show how influential someone might be to his followers. Also in Nigeria the way the media broadcasting Ebola, in TV, radio handbills and many more is so serious that even the opposition parties in the nation abandon polities to fight the disease. Everybody was seriously praying including the churches and mosques. The way they evangelize this Ebola myself was surprise, was it not because they don't want to die? For the first time all the contact number of Ebola was all working and the exception team also very active, why? Because it will affected them sooner or later. Therefore for Barrack Obama to say something and people follow it means that he is doing great things in the United States. Fulfilling destinies and realizing potentials because I know that any one that calls himself a leader and no one is following is taking a walk. But God is above all things whether president, minister or senator. God is the maker of destinies and protector of destinies and also making sure that those that trust in him fulfilled their destinies. Nothing happens on it own, but it is written

john 3:27

John answered and said, A man can receive nothing, except it be given him from heaven.

so whatever any man has; was given from heaven whether good or bad, Christians, Muslims, black, white, English or French all is given from [heaven]so there is no point or sense denying the God that supplies us with everything we have or need today. Some say they don't need God to succeed in their lives where as the breath is not theirs but God. I love God because he is full of mercies and compassionate

Roman 9:15-16

For he saith to Moses, I will have mercy on whom I will have mercy, and I will have compassion on whom I will have compassion.

16 So then it is not of him that willeth, nor of him that runneth, but of God that sheweth mercy.

If God were to be devil, earth will never be a dwelling place but God is not. God can be reasoned with, he said bring your strong reason together but the devil can never be reasoned with. If the Devil demand's anything from his captive's today, and fails to receive it, he kills the captive and possibly the family members as well and continues until God comes in. I have seen it happen.

Is really happening in short someone I knew in the street as a mad man was mad because according to the story, he went to a herbalist for help of making money but at the end the mother was demanded for the completion of the charm and he refuse, so madness became his possession. Why because if forgot the Words of the LORD that said give it shall be given unto you, pay your tithes

Malachi 3:8-12

Will a man rob God? Yet ye have robbed me. But ye say, Wherein have we robbed thee? In tithes and offerings.

9: Ye are cursed with a curse: for ye have robbed me, even this whole nation.

10: Bring ye all the tithes into the storehouse, that there may be meat in mine house, and prove me now herewith, saith the LORD of hosts, if I will not open you the windows of heaven, and pour you out a blessing, that there shall not be room enough to receive it.

11: And I will rebuke the devourer for your sakes, and he shall not destroy the fruits of your ground; neither shall your vine cast her fruit before the time in the field, saith the LORD of hosts.

12: And all nations shall call you blessed: for ye shall be a delightsome land, saith the LORD of hosts.

Then in

Philippians 4:10-19

But I rejoiced in the Lord greatly, that now at the last your care of me hath flourished again; wherein ye were also careful, but ye lacked opportunity.

11: Not that I speak in respect of want: for I have learned, in whatsoever state I am, therewith to be content.

12: I know both how to be abased, and I know how to abound: everywhere and in all things I am instructed both to be full and to be hungry, both to abound and to suffer need.

13: I can do all things through Christ which strengtheneth me.

14: Notwithstanding ye have well done, that ye did communicate with my affliction.

15: Now ye Philippians know also, that in the beginning of the gospel, when I departed from Macedonia, no church communicated with me as concerning giving and receiving, but ye only.

16: Now ye Philippians know also, that in the beginning of the gospel, when I departed from Macedonia, no church communicated with me as concerning giving and receiving, but ye only.

17: Not because I desire a gift: but I desire fruit that may abound to your account. 18:

But I have all, and abound: I am full, having received of Epaphroditus the things which were sent from you, an odour of a sweet smell, a sacrifice acceptable, wellpleasing to God.

19: But my God shall supply all your need according to his riches in glory by Christ Jesus.

We have to give to our pastors not because they need it but because they desire fruits that may abound to our accounts and the word **give** here is not only in money or to man but also to God. That is service in the house of God by participating in any activity that God is involve like ushering, electrical unit, sanctuary keeping and lots more. These are not money but strength. So no excuse not to give to God. it was the widows might that Jesus rated above all offering that day because that is all she had that day meaning your strength can certainly move God to your side. So there are opportunities in giving to God and pastors or anyone that is a spiritual head whether money or otherwise. The mad man never saw the advice of God and is not that he has never heard of it but unbelief and youthful lust consumed him and he went about believing in his friends and has now ended up picking papers in the streets.

...But my God shall supply all your need according to his riches in glory by Christ Jesus.

Never came if giving was not there. Anything you want is all over you but the lack of the knowledge my people perishes

HOSEA 4:6

My people are destroyed for lack of knowledge: because thou hast rejected knowledge, I will also reject thee, that thou shalt be no priest to me: seeing thou hast forgotten the law of thy God, I will also forget thy children.

Healing, honor, children, jobs, marriages all every other things that we may desire is all around only have the knowledge and believe. Knowledge is power therefore get a bible, read it and knows things concerning you and taking delivery of them. But if you don't have a bible and desire to have one ...please write to me, one will be send to you. There is nothing that is not in the bible. Yesterday is there, today is in it, and tomorrow is also there. Your name is there. Your problems and solutions are there too so why waste time in taking what is yours? People rather read magazines than reading the Word of God that is in the bible. Sometimes what matters in life doesn't matter to people because they lack the knowledge of truth. The things they don't set their hearts on are the things that destroy them. Those things that some called little things are the things that matters in most cases. Minor mistakes in French and English are the things that fail students in exam. Therefore put your hearts in the Word of God that is in the bible because salvation is there and through salvation we have all things. God knows why you are reading this so don't take it for granted he has the power to lunch you to your paradise within minutes. I ones had a friend, who knows all the Nollywood stars in Nigeria but ask her to quote a verse in the bible she cannot. Why? Because her church service ends only on a Sunday service after that no more opening of the bible to read. There are much people today in the world especially youths that when told that Jesus loves them they will say yeah I've heard it over and over again because my pastor said that every Sundays. But remember what the bible said in *PROVERBS 16:7*

When a man's ways please the LORD, he maketh even his enemies to be at peace with him.

It means when a man ways doesn't please God; the enemies of the man will never be at peace with him. And what is peace? Peace is been free from worry or bondage of any kind. So how can peace be when the things that matters to God does not matters to him. Therefore understand when the things that matters to God matters to man then the things that matter to man matters to God so if our things matters to God as his things matters to us, all our desires and all those things we could not ask or doubt will be given to us. Solomon asked for wisdom but God gave him wisdom, riches and honor because what matters to God matters to him. Also peace was also granted to him because throughout his reign in Israel there was no war. So God grant him peace because it is written, when a man's way please God, he [GOD] maketh his [man] enemies to be at peace with him. Obedience to God's principles makes us a principal to our principalities and what are his (God) principles? His Words! Written in Bible. So understand that obedience to God words is what curses the manifestation of God's blessings upon our lives. Remember that believing in God is very important because that is the only way that we can obtain that which he has promised and also a way of knowing who we really are on earth. Also all over the countries of the earth, there are the national identity cards, international passports where all the personal data of the bearer are and as much as a person has a national identity card, the identity of the person is known. Therefore identify yourself in Christ today and be among the people that will turn impossibility into cheap possibility

I pray that God takes you to your place of honor as you obey the Word of God and practice them. Amen

Finally unbelief should be eradicated from the minds of the youths today. And allow God to fight the battles whether Christian or Muslim because we are all the children of the most high whether black or white, English, French, Russia, Asia and Africa.

Sometime in April 2015,700 migrants died in the Mediterranean Sea while trying to cross to Europe. These 700 youths are all Africans that have been mislead with the illusion that Europe is the solution to their problems. My questions is ''IS AFRICANS SLAVES? And why are they easily mislead? I thought that slavery is over and is not longer permitted in the world today but till tomorrow there is still slavery among youths why? Today people are still caught for human trafficking and as a matter of fact, the unknown is higher than the known. African girls are been bought to be harlots in Europe, America, Australia, Asia and even some Africa countries as a matter of facts yet they say that there is nothing like slavery in the world. Well, my sympathy goes for the youths because they allowed it. Because I know for sure that how one dresses his bed so he lies on it.

I once met someone in Dubai and I ask him how is life here? Surprise he said nothing is happening here, in fact that he is just here because no choice. Now the question is "why would anyone be in a place where nothing is happening? Why will anyone believe that there is no choice? Is it not because he left home with desperation and lacks the knowledge of the kind of life people live there? That you must work before you eat? Therefore I plead to all the Heads of States, Presidents of African, Europe American, Asia, Australia to please send an aircraft to bring back anyone who is willing to go home and please let there be a offer attach to it. This offer may be a sum of money that can start up something in their respective home towns. I realize that many youths today are in foreign lands not because they want to remain there but because they see themselves worst than they were before and devil, been a deceiver, puts shame in their hearts .and for shame, they commit all manners atrocities in the land in which they found themselves. Also I appeal to other governments that have foreigners in their prisons to please grant them pardon and release them from prisons so that they can return to their respective lands.

Again am appealing to United Nations to please fish out this deceiver that dwells in Tunisia, Algeria, Morocco and Lybia and also strengthen their Government as to stop any illegal migration whether by Sea or Desert.

Nigeria is able to take care of her youths if she wishes to. Yes! Nigeria is very rich yet her youths go out to source for what they already had. But I thank God for the change that came to the nation.

Please understand that God chooses anybody to do His works on earth. During the presidential election in Nigeria, people were saying that Buhari will Islamatise Nigeria, just to pervert the will of God but they could not because God is not a man and the dove could not fly. The bible said in

Genesis 26v12-14

Then Isaac sowed in that land, and received in the same year an hundredfold: and the LORD blessed him.

13: And the man waxed great, and went forward, and grew until he became very great:

14: For he had possession of flocks, and possession of herds, and great store of servants: and the Philistines envied him.

This sowing is not a seed of faith or something that someone bought nor a package for pastors, church or even anything like money, car, house or anything givable but this sowing means hard work and diligence. So, in other words, Isaac work hard in that land and received in the same year an hundred fold: and the LORD bless him.

Please understand that working hard does not choose locations because the earth is the LORD'S and this LORD is everywhere, totally unlimited. Psalms24v1. Our God is limitless. Therefore I see absolutely no reason for any youth to settle for less when complete is possible.

I have seen and also heard from people what some youth does simply because they want to obtain papers to live in abroad; some went as far as selling their kidneys for money. Why? Because they believe that is a means of survivor. I always wonder why should a child of God that has much authority do such risky thing just to survive. I had said and will say, if any man wants to commit murder let him commit it himself than to lure innocent youths into it, may be taking advantage of their lack. For there is no election in Nigeria that youths don't die why? Is it not because of the money politicians make in the Government? Now cut down the cost of Governance and see if it will not stop because everybody will rather do business than been a politician and of course nobody wants to help others or sacrifice for others. Understand please that the youths are the future of the world therefore we cannot afford to be used for selfish purposes. I realize that for any nation to be successful, that nation must know how to manage her youths. Nigeria for example, has had two different issues because of mismanagement of her youths. Also, remember that that the world rebels are all in the mismanagement of youths. ISISI are 98% youths.

Now in Nigeria we have the Militants and the Boko Haran. But the militant was craftily managed and the Boko Haran is yet to be managed .but there is a way to solve terrorism problem permanently and Nigeria is too equipped and patient to suffer all that from BOKO HARAN though they have not known it.

See! Empowering youths is not just the answer, creating jobs is not the answer either though partly but also providing good environment and mentality through orientating them always because empowering somebody with a car for the purpose of taxi, without orientation that drinking and driving is counterproductive or leads to death, the empowerment will eventually becomes a curse.

Therefore I want to awaken the spirits of the youths of today and the generation to come, all over the world to be mindful of what they do and to recognize the purpose of God in their lives. Not to sale their Kidneys, bombs, assassinate, migrate illegally and many more things that the youths do these days. If there is a census in any country, the numbers of youths are always higher even when some are lock in prisons, some in overseas, in facts, there are police cells, prisons in Nigeria that people has been forgotten inside. There are people in prisons in Nigeria and other parts of the world that people have been forgotten. Let them be release because most of them are innocents, awaiting trial, envied, wickedness of people and much more. Image someone been on awaiting trial for 10years yet still lock up.

It is the responsibility of the youths to decide who becomes their leaders whether President or senators, Governor etc. because in a free and fair elections, the highest votes wins but not to be used as thugs to hijack ballots boxes, murder and stealing of all kinds.

Finally, getting papers to live in any nation does not warrant contract marriage, and going abroad by all means does not mean that you will be rich, Donating or giving out money to people to come to election campaign does not guarantee victory but do that which is right before God and man because whatever a man soweth, so shall he reap. If the Government will grant the youths pardon and will release them to go to their home towns, there will be to their amazements, lots of jobs, less crime rate and huge progress in the economy of that country. Below is a testimony of a brother almost deceived by these so called traveling agents and traveling abroad?

There was a promise by a traveling agent that with four hundred thousand [Nigeria] naira, he can work out visa for Greece and working permit attach. The 400 thousand was given but the visa was not found truthful because the agents forge a pilgrim visa to Mecca which he convince him that someone will pick him in Mecca and take him to Greece.. Finally, it never works out and the money was not refunded but after some years later, the victim became a business man. Now he is married with children. Successful in the same land he wanted running away from, a place he never thought possible. I pray that God should direct your heart to take good decisions in your life today and always in Jesus name Amen.

Chapter 3

UNBELIEF (LUKE 1V37)

Unbelief is a destroyer; unbelief is a waste of energy, fund and also a loss of lucrative opportunities. **Luke 1v37**

For with God nothing shall be impossible.

And after that,

45: **And blessed is she that believed: for there shall be a performance of those things which were told her from the Lord.** So believe has much to do in us, believe is the fast way to our solutions in life. Though there are several believes on this earth but there is a special and undeniable God that everybody should believe on because through him is salvation and life.

John11:20v40,

20:Then Martha, as soon as she heard that Jesus was coming, went and met him: but Mary sat still in the house.

21: Then said Martha unto Jesus, Lord, if thou hadst been here, my brother had not died.

22: But I know, that even now, whatsoever thou wilt ask of God, God will give it thee.

26: And whosoever liveth and believeth in me shall never die. Believest thou this?

27: She saith unto him, Yea, Lord: I believe that thou art the Christ, the Son of God, which should come into the world.

40: Jesus saith unto her, Said I not unto thee, that, if thou wouldest believe, thou shouldest see the glory of God?

Today some people don't believe in Christ Jesus, and some do believe in him but lack the understanding of his Words, and others believed in him as a Savior but not as a lord. Following Christ has to do with total submission to him in all areas of our lives. The bible said in **Phil 2:9-11**

Wherefore God also hath highly exalted him, and given him a name which is above every name:

10: That at the name of Jesus every knee should bow, of things in heaven, and things in earth, and things under the earth;

11: And that every tongue should confess that Jesus Christ is Lord, to the glory of God the Father... yet people don't believe in this powerful name. Please understand that it is what we believe that comes to us, therefore knowing what we believe on should be part of us. When Moses went to tell pharaoh to let Israel go, pharaoh said I know not your God neither will I let Israel go but at the end, he did let Israel go because he realize that in Gods case no appeal. Some people think that God is foolish therefore they do all manners of things hoping that God will not require it from them or at worse there is no God. Serving God and obeying his Words are for the interest of men not Gods because it transforms men but God remained the same forever. Some believe that, those that are not church members are better than the church goers because of the attitude of some church members but the truth here is that heavenly race is an individual race, not a group race but personal race and in bible **1cor.5v10**

Yet not altogether with the fornicators of this world, or with the covetous, or extortioners, or with idolaters; for then must ye needs go out of the world.

Believing in God should not come because your friend believe in God so will you, but because Jesus Christ is our Lord and personal savior. Also don't because of some certain mistakes of people stop worshiping, believing or going to churches because we will account for our own did not theirs. **Eccl12v13-14. Let us hear the conclusion of the whole matter: Fear God, and keep his commandments: for this is the whole duty of man. 14: For God shall bring every work into judgment, with every secret thing, whether it be good, or whether it be evil.**

Believing in God is not in words but by actions, that means living a live that is accepted by God, a holy and obedient live. Believing in God is not only by going to church, attending Christian meetings and partaking in every church activity. Though is part of our personal relationship with God and it matters. It doesn't matter how old is our Christianity or familiar we might be with the bible but how pleasing we are to God. Because some thought that Christianity is all about going to church and partaking in donation and some other church activities. Whereas their moral lives are not check, to them it seems their church activities have covered it. But here the bible said

Gal.6v4-7

6: But let every man prove his own work, and then shall he have rejoicing in himself alone, and not in another.

5: For every man shall bear his own burden.

6: Let him that is taught in the word communicate unto him that teacheth in all good things.

7: Be not deceived; God is not mocked: for whatsoever a man soweth, that shall he also reap.

What the bible meant here, is when doing something that relate to God we should make it personal because he is a God of personal. Don't do something you know is wrong because others are doing it, probably pastors, bishops, elders, priest etc is high way to the grave because even popes will appear before God. Please understand the strategy of the devil and try to live a life that will please God. For the devil has raise men to deceive people in churches, also discourage many from going to church to hear the Word of God. Because of what some ministers do, some people feel that there is no need of going to church or worshiping God. Because if them [ministers] with such office will act foolishly how much less those that only go to hear the Word, God does not recognize our tittles neither is he a respecter of any man. Please understand that when we refuse to worship God because of the attitudes of people, we are not doing ourselves any good but harm. also when we see a Christian going astray don't be deceive on what he or she is doing just know that God want us to come a little more closer to avoid us been tempted by the same spirit that is responsible for that one us saw.

Believing God should not be a burden to us. Accepting Christ is not difficult, is only by changing our mindset, putting worldly or earthly things away and set our mind on things above and also by putting off the old man and put on the new man.

Col.3v1-10.

If ye then be risen with Christ, seek those things which are above, where Christ sitteth on the right hand of God.

2: Set your affection on things above, not on things on the earth.

3: For ye are dead, and your life is hid with Christ in God.

4: When Christ, who is our life, shall appear, then shall ye also appear with him in glory.

5: Mortify therefore your members which are upon the earth; fornication, uncleanness, inordinate affection, evil concupiscence, and covetousness, which is idolatry:

6:For which things' sake the wrath of God cometh on the children of disobedience:

7: In the which ye also walked some time, when ye lived in them.

8: But now ye also put off all these; anger, wrath, malice, blasphemy, filthy communication out of your mouth.

9: Lie not one to another, seeing that ye have put off the old man with his deeds;

10: And have put on the new man, which is renewed in knowledge after the image of him that created him:

It is very important to accept Christ today in our heart and be free from all satanic entanglement. Accepting Christ is not loving our church members alone, is not helping the less privileged, not donations to the poor, but believing that Jesus Christ die for our sins and rose from the dead and he is alive forever more. For there are people that thinks that charity is the forgiveness of their sins.

Charity is good but not a spiritual exercise, forgiveness of sins is a spiritual thing where as charity is a physical thing. Please understand that because of unbelief several people has missed their blessings, healing and lots more. According to the bible, the people of Nazareth would not receive much signs and wonders of God because of unbelief.

Today in the lives of youths has been from one problem to another, moving to and fro looking for greener pastures. There has been a lot of death cases recorded as a result of migration. Many have died because of unbelief and some are living dead because of same unbelief. See! Existing and surviving are two different things. The problem is not in existence but in surviving because God has already made us in his own image. So the problem is surviving the race of life. The only way to survive in this life is by putting God first before any other thing in our lives because if he can give existence, he can much more ensure that we survive. Youths of today refuse to acknowledge God, refuse to know his ordinance and to keep them but choose to rebel against their maker by doing that which is pleased in their eyes. that is why there are lots of drugs addicts, immorality of various kinds in the lives of youths today. But the bible said **Prov.14v12**

> **There is a way which seemeth right unto a man, but the end thereof are the ways of death.**

> **eccl.12v1**

> **Remember now thy Creator in the days of thy youth, while the evil days come not, nor the years draw nigh, when thou shalt say, I have no pleasure in them;**

This is the era of the youths, the time when young youths will move the world, remember that Christ started his ministry at the age of 30 why didn't he wait till he turn 60? Listen, God doesn't call old people for ministry but young youths that still have strength to work.

> **Prov.27v4-5**

> **Wrath is cruel, and anger is outrageous; but who is able to stand before envy?**

> **5: Open rebuke is better than secret love.**

How can we use the strength given to us by God to do things that are vanity? Understand that the time of been old before serving God has past, Now is the time when youths will take over the affairs of the church of Christ, over the world as a whole because the strength is in us. You don't need to be old to have anointing because the authority has been given to you long ago see what the bible said in **mark16v15-18**

And he said unto them, Go ye into all the world, and preach the gospel to every creature.

16: He that believeth and is baptized shall be saved; but he that believeth not shall be damned.

17: And these signs shall follow them that believe; In my name shall they cast out devils; they shall speak with new tongues;

18: They shall take up serpents; and if they drink any deadly thing, it shall not hurt them; they shall lay hands on the sick, and they shall recover.

So you don't need to look like it, maybe being big, small, young or old does not guarantee the authority of God in your life but the genuine thirst and walk with God in personal basis.. Healing is possible with or without doctors yet people don't believe, prosperity is possible in Christ yet people are still in poverty. Christians for that matter. Listen, begging is an insult to Christendom. How can your father own riches and honor and the world in general yet you are languishing in poverty and shame.

2cor.8v9,

For ye know the grace of our Lord Jesus Christ, that, though he was rich, yet for your sakes he became poor, that ye through his poverty might be rich.

psalms24v1

The earth is the LORD's, and the fulness thereof; the world, and they that dwell therein.

Please note that riches are not in money or properties alone but also in health and marriage. The reason why people are still suffering today especially the youths is as a result of unbelief, not accepting their real selves. How can we know that we are like God?

Psalms82v6

I have said, Ye are gods; and all of you are children of the most High... and yet some allow someone to use them as an assassin because of money. If killing is good what stops him from killing the person himself? Why will we be the killer? Why will we campaign for someone to be elected wrongly or rig the election by carrying ballot boxes and other evil things for some one that will label us a suspect as soon as he or she is elected?

Don't we know that such people are called dirty jobs doers? And why will we be for dirty jobs? What happens to good jobs? As you see yourself so people take you. What stops them from using their sons and daughters for the dirty jobs? My friend we are made by the image of God not to be used as a ram like an outcast, a worthless thing because of money. Why should it be me whenever there is evil i will be the first to be Informed? The word dignity is it for special people or a choice? Nobody is big and nobody is small, is all about ourselves and our beliefs.

Believing in GOD is the best thing that can happen to any man because it will really ease your life. The reason why Thomas Edison took 99 experiments to get light in a bulb was because he was been judge by work but in the case of those that absolutely depends on God will never be the same because of the gift of grace

Roman 11v5-6

Even so then at this present time also there is a remnant according to the election of grace.

6: And if by grace, then is it no more of works: otherwise grace is no more grace. But if it be of works, then it is no more grace: otherwise work is no more work.

believing in God is the right thing to do as a human being because by believe you live a life without fears and sickness because he whom you believe has borne your grief's and by his stripes you are made whole. Healed

Isaiah53v4-5

Surely he hath borne our griefs, and carried our sorrows: yet we did esteem him stricken, smitten of God, and afflicted.

5: But he was wounded for our transgressions, he was bruised for our iniquities: the chastisement of our peace was upon him; and with his stripes we are healed.

Some say that there is God and others say that there is no God but what is the bible said?

Genesis1v1

In the beginning God created the heaven and the earth.

Means that is God that created heaven and the earth. some say that if truly that there is God why is all the evil happening on earth today? It is written in the book of

Matthew 24v3-7

And as he sat upon the mount of Olives, the disciples came unto him privately, saying, Tell us, when shall these things be? and what shall be the sign of thy coming, and of the end of the world?

4: And Jesus answered and said unto them, Take heed that no man deceive you.

6 And ye shall hear of wars and rumours of wars: see that ye be not troubled: for all these things must come to pass, but the end is not yet.

7 For nation shall rise against nation, and kingdom against kingdom: and there shall be famines, and pestilences, and earthquakes, in divers places.

also some say I don't believe in Jesus Christ because he is a tale for grown children and other said I am a theologies am 40 year old Christian therefore I know all about Christ Jesus, Jesus Christ is real, heaven is real, hell is real, blessing is real, cursing is real, preserving is real and destruction is real **matthew 16v13-16**

> **When Jesus came into the coasts of Caesarea Philippi, he asked his disciples, saying, Whom do men say that I the Son of man am?**
>
> **14: And they said, Some say that thou art John the Baptist: some, Elias; and others, Jeremias, or one of the prophets.**
>
> **15: He saith unto them, But whom say ye that I am?**
>
> **16: And Simon Peter answered and said, Thou art the Christ, the Son of the living God.**

The problem with some people is over reading of books. Note what the bible said in **Eccl 12v12**

> **And further, by these, my son, be admonished: of making many books there is no end; and much study is a weariness of the flesh.**

Meaning there is a limit to study. Please understand that many books inform but only the bible transforms yet millions of youths today that looks for greener pastures don't have it. In the Word of God there are riches and honor, there are healing and cure, there are protection and preservation and all we can ever want for ourselves. Youths travel from one place to the other searching for what is around them and many a time they die trying to migrate to a place they believe that is filled with milk and honey but hear this, there is no free meal in free town. There is nothing like that, no such thing like free meal. If you must know, there are people in the country we want to go that we are better with in financial matter so why risk your life trying to get to a place that you will be hunted by the police and other crimes agents? You think all stories are true? don't be deceived by the depression we face at times, you will make it better in your home land if you believe in the LORD of Hosts, JEHOVAH and after that you will go to the country of your choice in grand style not smuggling yourself into a place making yourself a fugitive where as you are not, see any one that say that there is no God is only jealous of God and is suffering from deepest depression therefore it is important to know that there is God and he cares for our well fare .

Some people are offended by God. They are angry with God maybe because their expectation was not granted immediately or their hope on the wrong thing so they became angry with God. understand that heaven and hell is real whether people believe it or not whether they compare God with a man or not because some say why will a loving father destroy his own son with fire but they forgot that it was written and God is not a man.

Number23v19

God is not a man, that he should lie; neither the son of man, that he should repent: hath he said, and shall he not do it? or hath he spoken, and shall he not make it good?

He has done it before with water. Hear! People that loves going where they will tell them sweet things, will end up where bitter thing were. So know that those type of people that receive **"you are bless"** from pastors yet their life is not blessed then they have problem with God because the word spoken out of the mouth of the pastors can be deceptive but the LORD can never be. so understand that you are bless in your finance, marriages and jobs spoken by pastors is not a guarantee to be bless whether it is spoken by pope himself or not but by the will of God concerning the receiver plus the attitude he or she show towards God because pope, pastors, Bishops or apostle are all chosen by God and they all are subjected to the will of God. If a murderer went to a priest and deceive him to pray for him so that when he go out to search for his victims he will meet them in a convenient place (though he might not tell him exactly) and the priest pray and said O LORD let the desire of this man be granted. Will God grant it? No, because the man has deceived man and not God. The bible said when the 70 men Jesus sent to preach returned and was celebrating because they heal the sick, raise the dead and cast out devils but Jesus said to them rejoice not in all these things but that your name is written in the book of life meaning that there is book of death. Heaven is a home hell is a home, both is a choice. What is your choice?

Exodus14v14

The LORD shall fight for you, and ye shall hold your peace.

Is not for unbelievers,

Jeremiah33v3-6

3: Call unto me, and I will answer thee, and shew thee great and mighty things, which thou knowest not.

4 :For thus saith the LORD, the God of Israel, concerning the houses of this city, and concerning the houses of the kings of Judah, which are thrown down by the mounts, and by the sword;

5: They come to fight with the Chaldeans, but it is to fill them with the dead bodies of men, whom I have slain in mine anger and in my fury, and for all whose wickedness I have hid my face from this city.

6: Behold, I will bring it health and cure, and I will cure them, and will reveal unto them the abundance of peace and truth.

Is not for unbelievers,

Exodus 23v25-26

And ye shall serve the LORD your God, and he shall bless thy bread, and thy water; and I will take sickness away from the midst of thee.

26: There shall nothing cast their young, nor be barren, in thy land: the number of thy days I will fulfil. Is never for unbelievers,

Job22v29

When men are cast down, then thou shalt say, There is lifting up; and he shall save the humble person.

Is not for unbelievers

Psalms 113v7-9

He raiseth up the poor out of the dust, and lifteth the needy out of the dunghill;

8:That he may set him with princes, even with the princes of his people.

9 He maketh the barren woman to keep house, and to be a joyful mother of children. Praise ye the LORD.

Is not for unbelievers.

All things are possible to them that believe not to them that believeth not. No matter the exploits we do on earth please try that your name is written in the book of life because that is the ultimate and the trophy of the race of life. Whether pastors, deacons, Bishops elders, no matter the miracles and the fame

Make sure your name is written in the book of life because without it, your labor is in vain. Is because of unbelief that makes people to remain in sickness even in churches today. I watch a live programmed where a lady was interviewing someone, a lady also and she said that she has only 2weeks to live and started crying, that her disease was incurable. Please I am one of the people that have once said they will die in a certain time in *2003* and this book is in *2014* that I got the vision and also wrote it. So you can put scores yourself. Please if you are given date to live maybe because of illness or any forms of the devices of the devil just come to me let me lead you to Christ whom is live and pray with you in faith and believe that Jesus has heal you. When I lead you to Christ and Christ takes place in your life then I will see the devil that will take live that Jesus has given you. If you have relatives or friends that the doctor has given days or weeks to live just contact me he or she will live before the very face of the verdict even the doctors will be surprise and they will know that God is the maker of heaven and earth. Any one that died sick in the house of God is a disgrace to Christianity. How can they hear that Christ is the balm of Gilead yet some are sick .it means that they don't believe in the God they called? That is what I called sheep's in wolf clothing's and how can they believe when their heart is not with God, how can their heart be with God when they are religious people? And why will they not be religious people when they go to churches just to cover their wickedness pretending to serve God. And why will they serve God when they believe in their riches and technology and all the wisdom of men including herbalist, witchcrafts. And at the end hell becomes a home. I pray that every devil deceiving people in churches today catch fire in Jesus name Amen.

If you want something better in your life-you can have it! If you want something better in health you can have it! If you want all your bills paid up you can have it! If doctors say you have two weeks to live you can see old age! If you want your unsaved loved ones saved God can do it. Whatever your situation may be now God has something better for you if you only believed. Don't blame God for your situation. Many people blame their lack of success and prosperity on God "I'm poor, defeated because its Gods will" but that is not true,

3 john 2

Beloved, I wish above all things that thou mayest prosper and be in health, even as thy soul prospereth.

Believing in God is not through word but through action by obedience.

In *john2 vs3-11*

And when they wanted wine, the mother of Jesus saith unto him, They have no wine.

4 Jesus saith unto her, Woman, what have I to do with thee? mine hour is not yet come.

5: His mother saith unto the servants, Whatsoever he saith unto you, do it.

6: And there were set there six waterpots of stone, after the manner of the purifying of the Jews, containing two or three firkins apiece.

7: Jesus saith unto them, Fill the waterpots with water. And they filled them up to the brim.

8:And he saith unto them, Draw out now, and bear unto the governor of the feast. And they bare it. 9:When the ruler of the feast had tasted the water that was made wine, and knew not whence it was: (but the servants which drew the water knew;) the governor of the feast called the bridegroom, 10:And saith unto him, Every man at the beginning doth set forth good wine; and when men have well drunk, then that which is worse: but thou hast kept the good wine until now.

11, This beginning of miracles did Jesus in Cana of Galilee, and manifested forth his glory; and his disciples believed on him.

Now if the mother of Jesus did not believe in him, she would not have gone to him. Also the servants wouldn't have filled the pots if they had not believed. So obedience is a part of believe. So the servants obeyed they believe and if they had not believed in Jesus, shame would have been their portion that very day. Believing in God should also show in our attitudes towards God and man, in the bible, John the Baptist was offended by Christ and the end result cost him his life. Believing in God needs a good character towards your beliefs because without the right attitude failure is inevitable. In my search to get a better definition of live, the secrets to success in life both carnally and spiritually. I realize a mathematical expression of success.

If	A	B	C	D	E	F	G	H	I	J	K	L	M	N	O	P	Q	R	S	T	U	V	W	X	Y	Z
	1	2	3	4	5	6	7	8	9	10	11	12	13	14	15	16	17	18	19	20	21	22	23	24	25	26

Then, what makes our live success?

H	A	R	D	W	O	R	K	?		K	N	O	W	L	E	D	G	E?
8	1	18	4	23	15	18	11	= 98%		11	14	15	23	12	5	4	7	5 = 96%

L	O	V	E?		L	U	C	K	?		M	O	N	E	Y?
12	15	22	5 = 54%		12	21	3	11	= 47%		13	15	14	5	25 = 72%

None of them makes 100%
What makes 100%???

L	E	A	D	E	R	S	H	I	P
12	5	1	4	5	18	19	8	9	16 = 97%

Every problem has a solution, only if we perhaps change our Attitude.

A	T	T	I	T	U	D	E
1	20	20	9	20	21	4	5 = 100%

So it is therefore our attitude towards life, God and work that makes our life 100% successful. Therefore stay away from anger, because it hurts only you. If you are right then there is no need to be angry, if are wrong you have no right to be angry.

Patience with family is love

Patience with others is respect

Patience with self is confidence

Patience with God is faith.

Never think more about the past it brings TEARS......

Never think more about the future it brings FEARS.......

Live this moment with a smile it brings cheer.

People get angry when an expectation is not met but forgets that every problem comes to make us or break us, the choice is ours whether we become victims or victorious. Beautiful things are not always good but good things are beautiful. Happiness keeps you sweet but being sweet brings happiness. Often we complain about life and the negative things that happen to us, forgetting that everything happens for a purpose. I read a story about a man who was a song writer and a successful Christian lawyer Heratio Stafford who's only son died at the age of (4) four in 1871, in 1872 the great Chicago fire wiped out his vest estate made from a successful legal career, in 1873 lost his four (4) daughters who were on a summer trip to Europe. His law firm was burned down and the insurance refused to pay, they said "it's an act of God" he also lost his house and work but one day while sitting and thinking about what was happening to him, and as a spiritual person, he wrote a song – whatever my LORD thou has taught me to say – it is well, it is well with my soul. My friends you see a good attitude will determine your altitude. What have you lost in life? What is that mountain you think you cannot climb? When you look at your life, career, job or family what do you see? When doctors tell you, you have a heart disease, what do you say? When every light seems to be turned off, and your life seems dark, what do you say? Do you praise God or blame him? Do you blame yourself or the devil? A good attitude towards God makes him move on your favor. Just say it is well with my soul, I am thankful I had a peaceful sleep, I am thankful I am alive with possibilities, I am thankful I have a job, family and friends and above all I have Jesus Christ on my side, be thankful because your starting point is someone's end point target. There was a day I had only fifty Nigeria naira (₦ 50) with me, someone came and asked me for that money, I gave it to him and that was how he was able to eat that day. Thank God for what you have, no matter what you are going through today believe God and thank him for it, then you will see God working on your behalf, ending everything that brings sorrow to your life. Please don't complain like john the Baptist, because he believed that he has done much for Christ even as his cousin, therefore Christ should abandon his ministry and go deliver him from prison. Forgetting that Christ whom was also his cousin raised Lazarus from the dead after four days and he also knew that john was in prison and would have gone for his rescue that day but john the Baptist murmured and asked if he was the one that was supposed to come or if they should wait for another. Finally he was beheaded. See, unbelief is a killer, if john the Baptist had believed and had got a good attitude towards Jesus Christ he wouldn't have been beheaded at that time. I've seen lots of people asking me lots of questions "are you sure that there is God? And if there is, does he know me? Why does he not know my name and address? Why will I be like this? Why did he take the only thing that I have? Why did he allow my family to die in car crash to be among the one that was burnt? I have been regular in church I partook in every activity both momentarily and otherwise, why did God allow my only son to die? Am I not an elder in the church? Doing God's work diligently and he allowed my daughters to die in a plane crash. All these questions are wrong attitude towards God. Pope or pastors, deacon or member even apostles none is greater than God. The story of **job** in the bible from chapter 1 – 42 was to tell Christians that affliction may come but the end is good. Some of these evil happens because of our inability to be sensitive in the realm of the spirit because God speaks to us.

Job 33:14-18

For God speaketh once, yea twice, yet man perceiveth it not.

15:In a dream, in a vision of the night, when deep sleep falleth upon men, in slumberings upon the bed;

16:Then he openeth the ears of men, and sealeth their instruction,

17:That he may withdraw man from his purpose, and hide pride from man.

18:He keepeth back his soul from the pit, and his life from perishing by the sword.

Therefore God is not to be blamed for any loss that we may experience in life. Recently I received a call that someone had died while in labor. First I was not told that she was pregnant nor was I told that she will be delivering. It was after her death and entry in the mortuary that I was told about it. Now is the death caused by God? No, but their ignorance, if they had been sensitive in the spirit, they would have know when God revealed it to them, if they had gone to church or even pray, God would have given them the solution to the problems they were facing, but they relaxed and slept while the devil and his agents were working, seeking, whom to kill, steal and destroy. There are wickedness in the highest order the bible said it in

Eccl 8:11

Because sentence against an evil work is not executed speedily, therefore the heart of the sons of men is fully set in them to do evil.

In some parts of the world, wickedness is higher than others. A woman will be pregnant some enemies will want her dead or prolong the duration of her pregnancy; I have seen a woman whom is three years pregnant. Some people do not build houses in their villages because they are afraid to die, some do not drive their cars to the village because they are afraid that people may kill them. You answer more questions in the classroom you are in trouble because some people think that you are showing that you're more intelligent than the others. Knowing God is important, though there are gods but there is a God and his name is JEHOVAH, the father of our Lord Jesus Christ whom is above all other gods. So know now that the choice you make will determine your end. Please understand that life is not a funfair but a warfare, therefore it is very important to identify yourself in the kingdom of the living God and end sorrows, sickness and disgraced forever, and you will be free from all manner of harassment from the devil when you identify yourself you rise above devil and his agents above all oppressions of the kingdom of darkness.

Now it is so sad to know that people complain about God and celebrate devil, in sickness, poverty, academically and otherwise. Remember that devil is the chancellor in the University of Lies, a PHD holder in lies but is so sad that people now believe Satan than God. They believe pain rather than peace. sickness rather than health.

3john2

Beloved, I wish above all things that thou mayest prosper and be in health, even as thy soul prospereth.

Yet someone said that he is sick. I once heard a young lady saying I have migraine. Some say they have cancer, heart diseases, brain tumor and incurable disease and diabetes. These are all lies of the devil and people are believing it and confessing it daily and because the scripture cannot be broken it will be so to them that confesses it. It is written that there is power in spoken words

*proverb13:3*He that keepeth his mouth keepeth his life: but he that openeth wide his lips shall have destruction.

therefore you are sick because you said so and accepted it, if you say within you NO that you are not sick then you are not sick because the bible says "let the weak say I am strong, let the poor say I am rich "so say now that you are not sick and see if that demon called sickness will not let you be. The bible said life and death is in spoken words. So start speaking life and good and see it manifesting in Jesus name. Speak the impossible because your God is a specialist in making the impossible possible, and he has given you the power to do the same. There is a state in Nigeria that has international recognition for tourism because of the famous carnival. This carnival which usually took place on 26th and 27th of every December has huge influences in the lives of the admirers and tourist. This carnival attracts much people coming from all over the nation and beyond to the state. But I believe that there is something that people is yet to know concerning the carnival. One of the Governors of the state was probably thinking of how to move the state forward and instead of building industries and factories he choose carnivals reasons best known to him and went as far as signing it as a law, that it must be celebrated every year.

So our nation gathers together to drink, smoke, commit fornication, adultery and unconsciously worshiping what they don't know because they don't know the mind of the Governor that introduced such thing because nothing goes for anything. Please understand that nothing is ordinary, there is always a price for everything whether good or bad

See! In every gathering, it's either is for God or for Satan and am very certain that it is not for God because God never encourage women walking half naked.

Now poverty is taken care of them in so much that if it were possible they will want God to pay tax because all the oil-wells of the state has been taken. Cameroon took some; their neighboring state took the rest. Now they believe that the carnival is the solutions to their pains because of the little money that they make out of it where as carnival is the head of their problem, therefore they are the reason of their hardships. They now go by the name "civil servant state" what happen when all the oil-wells were there? Were not the oil-wells there before the governor come? Why did it go after the initiation of the carnival? See! When the children of Israel disobeyed God, God drive them to another land to serve men and be captives and as soon as they return to God, God will bring them back again to the place which he has kept for them. This is exactly the problem of this state in Nigeria.

Jeremiah5v19-31

And it shall come to pass, when ye shall say, Wherefore doeth the LORD our God all these things unto us? then shalt thou answer them, Like as ye have forsaken me, and served strange gods in your land, so shall ye serve strangers in a land that is not your's.

20: Declare this in the house of Jacob, and publish it in Judah, saying,

21: Hear now this, O foolish people, and without understanding; which have eyes, and see not; which have ears, and hear not:

22: Fear ye not me? saith the LORD: will ye not tremble at my presence, which have placed the sand for the bound of the sea by a perpetual decree, that it cannot pass it: and though the waves thereof toss themselves, yet can they not prevail; though they roar, yet can they not pass over it?

23: But this people hath a revolting and a rebellious heart; they are revolted and gone.

24: Neither say they in their heart, Let us now fear the LORD our God, that giveth rain, both the former and the latter, in his season: he reserveth unto us the appointed weeks of the harvest.

25: Your iniquities have turned away these things, and your sins have withholden good things from you.

26: For among my people are found wicked men: they lay wait, as he that setteth snares; they set a trap, they catch men.

27: As a cage is full of birds, so are their houses full of deceit: therefore they are become great, and waxen rich.

28: They are waxen fat, they shine: yea, they overpass the deeds of the wicked: they judge not the cause, the cause of the fatherless, yet they prosper; and the right of the needy do they not judge.

29: Shall I not visit for these things? saith the LORD: shall not my soul be avenged on such a nation as this?

30: A wonderful and horrible thing is committed in the land;

31: The prophets prophesy falsely, and the priests bear rule by their means; and my people love to have it so: and what will ye do in the end thereof?

I pray that the youths understand this and the Holy Spirit enlighten the eyes of their understanding to know what they carry, and be able to do them and also the things that the devil has stolen from them, God will restore seven fold back to them.

Proverbs6v31

But if he be found, he shall restore sevenfold; he shall give all the substance of his house.

See! Devil is the a thief, he is responsible for all the troubles of your life, all the barrenness, lack, shame, sickness, pains, marriage and all other manner of troubles that you have face in life. **john10v10The thief cometh not, but for to steal, and to kill, and to destroy: I am come that they might have life, and that they might have it more abundantly. .** Therefore he has to pay, through your realizing that he is the one that has stolen your joy. and going to God in prayers and supplication and all the days of your life will be filled with joy because all that you have lost will be restored and you will live above Satan and his agents. Please note that people who are ashamed of God (Jesus Christ) will not benefit much from him. I realize that today's youth are ashamed of God; they don't want to be seen with the bible or be called a born again Christian but a time is coming when Christianity will be like a competition because everybody will want to be identified as a Christian. So understand that there is benefit in worshiping God, if not, people all over the world wouldn't be worshiping God. Imagine people like Benny Hymns, Billy graham, Kenneth E Hagin. David Oyedepo, Pastor Adebayo, T D JAKE worshiping God. Worshiping God is for our own benefits not God because God can't not be sick, lack, confuse or worry, even problems in marriage he can't. But we have all these problems, we need good health, to be fill, protected and all other good things of life **job36v11If they obey and serve him, they shall spend their days in prosperity, and their years in pleasures.** God said he has not called the seed of Jacob to seek him in vain, meaning there are blessings attached in seeking God. **Jeremiah3v13-15Only acknowledge thine iniquity, that thou hast transgressed against the LORD thy God, and hast scattered thy ways to the strangers under every green tree, and ye have not obeyed my voice, saith the LORD.14Turn, O backsliding children, saith the LORD; for I am married unto you: and I will take you one of a city, and two of a family, and I will bring you to Zion: 15And I will give you pastors according to mine heart, which shall feed you with knowledge and understanding.** though you might have accomplished some of your dreams that makes you a successful person but no matter how successful you might be, you still have dreams and ambitions that are yet to be fulfilled and potentials as well. I pray that God fill you with spirit of wisdom, understanding and knowledge in Jesus name Amen. Is only God that can make your dreams come through? I watch a documentary in BBC, a mother lose her son who was trying to migrate to united state of America through desert unfortunately lost his life in the desert. Also another lady was being interviewed about her zeal to cross to united state and she said that she has tried 5 times and not been able but yet she won't give up. Unbelief has curse a lot of deaths to the youth today. Many youths has died while trying to migrate illegally to Europe and America. Some through sea and some through land (deserts). But the question here is "is there any tree that grows money on it In Europe or America? No. Is there money on the streets of America or Europe that people pick while walking? No. the people of America or Europe and other parts of the world that people rush to, do they work to get their money or they wait for manner to fall from heaven? They work. The people that own the place that other people hope to work when they get there, do they acquire them in foreign land or in their home lands? They acquire them in their home lands. Do you think everybody is rich in America or Europe? What then makes some people risk their lives in trying to get there? Unbelief plus ignorance. When they get there, will they not work as of other country which there is inclusive? They do. Or is there free meal in America or Europe? No, even in free town there is no free meal. If no employment, is there laws that stops people from doing business of their own? No. what is the difference between people and Bill gate whose wealth was not from natural resources? Commitment. I through the privilege of God has gone some places in the world and I have never seen or heard that there is a tree that grows money in them nor saw money in the streets of America or Europe that people pick while walking rather they in Europe and America work very hard for money. So why the risk of going where working for money is inevitable? Where as you can work in your land and still be successful. Please note, going to America or Europe is not bad if it genuine but not engaging in an act that may cost lives Just because you want to migrate to another nation as I saw in BBC and in case you want the privilege I had, just called on Jesus Christ today and you will receive more grace than I have. The bible said whatever a man soweth same shall he reap.

Meaning whatever you sow whether in your land or oversea you will reap it. But sow comes before reaping. It is written seed time and harvest will not cease **Genesis8v22While the earth remaineth, seedtime and harvest, and cold and heat, and summer and winter, and day and night shall not cease.** seed time and harvest. Meaning that is only God that determined the harvest time. Therefore sow where ever you and God is there to make a nation out of you **Genesis26v1-14And there was a famine in the land, beside the first famine that was in the days of Abraham. And Isaac went unto Abimelech king of the Philistines unto Gerar. 2And the LORD appeared unto him, and said, Go not down into Egypt; dwell in the land which I shall tell thee of: 3Sojourn in this land, and I will be with thee, and will bless thee; for unto thee, and unto thy seed, I will give all these countries, and I will perform the oath which I sware unto Abraham thy father; 4And I will make thy seed to multiply as the stars of heaven, and will give unto thy seed all these countries; and in thy seed shall all the nations of the earth be blessed;5Because that Abraham obeyed my voice, and kept my charge, my commandments, my statutes, and my laws.6And Isaac dwelt in Gerar: 12Then Isaac sowed in that land, and received in the same year an hundredfold: and the LORD blessed him. 13And the man waxed great, and went forward, and grew until he became very great: 14For he had possession of flocks, and possession of herds, and great store of servants: and the Philistines envied him.** it does not matter where you are or who you are, nobody came with money to the earth when God create Adam and eve they were without money until God gave them. There was no money on earth when God created it, but God gave man the wisdom to create something that will be generally accepted as means of exchange. So you can make something too that will launch you to the top and make you a symbol of blessing to your generation and generation to come. God knows why you are reading this book today, he has seen you struggling and he want to put an end to it by making you realize that America, Europe, Asia and every other parts of this world is just a place in earth and that they can fail but he cannot fail.

Therefore don't put your trust in America or Europe but believe that God can do anything you want. Remember when there is a need, there is a miracle. There is no free food, house or car there you have to buy anything you want or need so why the risk of illegal migration? Please understand that life is not a fun fare but warfare and the battle ground is the heart. If we can win the thoughts of our heart, then the battle is won. Note that, as long as you believe that you cannot prosper in your countries, the power of believe or thoughts will start working against you to ensure that your thoughts come to pass.

Chapter 4

SUCIDE

This is a means in which the devil used to populate his kingdom. This is the system which Satan think is the best way to destroyed the youths of today. The major problem of man is ungratefulness and lack of knowledge because if man had known that the end of a thing is better than the beginning; there will be less crimes and death cases in the world today. Therefore, it is always good to be grateful at all times because you are what the world is waiting for. How can someone created by God take his own life? Simply because he lacks the understanding of whom he is. See! You are the leader of tomorrow, you have the potentials of a leader therefore use them to change lives on earth. Character is what determines the levels of someone's success. I pray that you will not make a wrong turn in your life in Jesus name Amen. Money is not all you need to succeed because much has succeeded without money at the first stage of their lives. Good characters and ideas is grater and better than money, knowledge in the other hand is richer because without knowledge nothing is possible; no matter how big it can be, it cannot be utilized to create anything, but with knowledge a trillion dollar is possible. Therefore knowledge is what is needed in youth age. All things are possible through Christ whether riches, health, life, marriage, and babies it is all possible through the knowledge of Jesus Christ. God is a respecter of his Words because his Words is him

john 1:1In the beginning was the Word, and the Word was with God, and the Word was God. according to the book of **Isaiah**

55:8-11For my thoughts are not your thoughts, neither are your ways my ways, saith the LORD. 9: For as the heavens are higher than the earth, so are my ways higher than your ways, and my thoughts than your thoughts. 10: For as the rain cometh down, and the snow from heaven, and returneth not thither, but watereth the earth, and maketh it bring forth and bud, that it may give seed to the sower, and bread to the eater: 11: So shall my word be that goeth forth out of my mouth: it shall not return unto me void, but it shall accomplish that which I please, and it shall prosper in the thing whereto I sent it. then in **3john 2, Beloved, I wish above all things that thou mayest prosper and be in health, even as thy soul prospereth.** Understand that whatever the LORD has said he is able to do it. Starting small is the best way to greatness in life because nothing is big without big mistakes. Thinking is the largest resources guided by God if allowed, thinking is the fastest way of getting ideas, and am not talking about the thinking in **matt 6:25 which says, .. Take no thought for your life, what ye shall eat, or what ye shall drink; nor yet for your body, what ye shall put on. Is not the life more than meat, and the body than raiment? ..** But creative thinking just likes a research. It was in thinking that God gave the idea of how man can create several things today. It is very important for youths to think on how to create and help others. I have said it before that problem either makes us better or destroy us but the good news is that problem gives us the choice to choose whether it will destroy or make us better. Understand that problem is a part of life, without it life would be incomplete. Remember that God created man to solve problems not problems to kill man or man kill himself because of problem. **Gen1:26. And God said, Let us make man in our image, after our likeness: and let them have dominion over the fish of the sea, and over the fowl of the air, and over the cattle, and over all the earth, and over every creeping thing that creepeth upon the earth.**

Having dominion is to solve the problem of the earth. Then **gen2:15 And the LORD God took the man, and put him into the garden of Eden to dress it and to keep it.** to dress it and keep it is also a duty, which is also a problem to be solved. Therefore the purpose of God creating man is to worship him and to solve problems of the earth. Some people feel that the world will be better without them so they believe that death is a friend, because of depression and confusion, so they believe that suicides is the solution to the problem they face on earth. though not that they really want to end their lives but there sufferings that makes them feel worthless and having no reason to live. Please understand that God knows everything about us, everything that concerns us concerns God, anything that we might be going through he knows all of it.

Suicide is foolishness, ignorance of the highest other. It's only a foolish man that would want to build a house in one day yet some people wants to end their suffering in a minute.

No matter how distressing our circumstances maybe, even the ones that are beyond our control as man, is not worth committing suicide. Suicide has been in recent years a means Satan has used to draw souls to himself.

Please understand there are things that man cannot change, and when such thing comes learn to cope with them rather than inviting pride to ourselves. I realize that much people have died because of pride. How can I live like this? It is better to die than to go to jail, am rich before but now I cannot even buy a pair of shoes, all of these are frustrating ideas that stir up the spirit of suicide simply because you want to conceal or end a problem, finally turns to a curse because the bible said "curse to any man that hang on a tree". I have never seen anyone celebrated for committing suicide, there is always a way out of every problem because God has never allowed any problem to kill man because he always provides a way of escape. If they live and work on their emotions, surely they will live to see how that very problem will turn into a testimony. I am very certain that all the fears will turn into testimonies, understand that thinking much about the past brings tears and sorrows even regrets and also brings stupid ideas especially when the past was bad. Thinking much about the future brings fears. live every moment with cheer, remember that every test in our life makes us better or bitter. every problem comes to make us or break us, the choice is always ours whether we become victims or victorious. Please note that there are no short cuts to solutions of life other than Jesus Christ.

2Corinth 4:8We are troubled on every side, yet not distressed; we are perplexed, but not in despair; some turn to alcoholic for solution and some to tobaccos and hard drug but all to no avail. Alcohol, tobacco and any hard drugs even suicide that are being imagined is twice as bad as acting it physically because the former state is always better than the latter state, but there is a cure to depression, mental confusion, drugs addiction, tuition fees, miracles, healing, deliverance, marriage, babies, jobs, and many more, this cure has been tested and approved by God and I am one of the beneficiary, this cure has turned a nonentity to a celebrity, changes HIV&AIDS positive to negative, turn poverty to success, restore sanity, break barriers and much more and this unfaultable cure is PRAISE. It might look foolish but try it just praise God for the duration of three days and see for yourself. Praise God today and see the wonder of praise, praise him with your voice, with your dance, with a clap. Please understand that your voice doesn't have to be the best before you praise God, you must not know how to dance before you dance for God. Do things that you have not done for God in praise and I assure you, you will suddenly call me to share your testimony and I'm waiting for your call, when you'll say "I thought it is foolishness but I tried it behold am free". Note! The foolishness of God is wiser than man; also understand also that you can use a gospel song or tape in case you don't know what to sing and language is not a barrier either. Therefore you can use any language of your choice to praise God and you will never regret doing it, in fact it will become a solution for others throughout your life time. For a start take three days and praise God on what you want him to do and what he has done, you will be amaze to see that all the things you want will start coming on their own accord, praise has restored a menstrual circle of seven month of no menstruation of a lady, it put confusion in the camps of the enemies, remember, when you dance you don't just entertain but provoking God to do what you want. Please understand that is doesn't take God a year to turn your life around, it takes your praise when you want to see the manifestation of God in your life, the best thing to do is to bring God down through praise. Praise is a wrestling ring where when one is tired, goes to bet another in the other team in the ring. God works wonders through praise, praise is the moving force of the world of no limit. Alcohol, drugs, suicide can never delivered anyone from pains but by praise. My pastor shared a testimony with us how when he want to add a degree to himself so he went to his brothers and sisters even relatives for help but none gave him the help he needed. That night he engage in praise, he praise god all through the night than in the next day morning while walking to school someone called him and ask "I heard that you have not paid your school fees and how much is the fees? And that was how the man drove him (my pastor) to his office and gave him the tuition fees. But the surprising thing according to the man who later became a pastor (my pastor) which is my pastor is that the man was a Muslim not evens a Christian. So God can use anybody to meet your needs just praise God today and live to testify his glorious works and acts.

Once I had meet someone while traveling and when we got to the city, people started dropping their bus stops but mine was a little further, the boy said I will drop here, I will drop there so I realized he doesn't have where he was going to so I said come with me to my house maybe God will provide for you a place, after four days he got a job in a hotel and it happened that the owner of the hotel is a member of the church where i worship. so trust and confidence where much on him then the spirit of cheating took over him and he started cheating his co – staffs and at the end he was sacked. The boy once told me that it's better for him to die because he has suffered enough; he made me to believe all his lies and even saying that there is no God. I was very determined to help him. But finally he betrayed himself. So many times if we search well, we will discover that we are the problems that we have not necessarily the devil. This boy said something about dying which makes me want to help and to prove him wrong that there is God but his character could not let him. Why want to kill yourself when you can simply change your character, your attitude towards things. Why not let go of those people who always sees wrongs in you. Why not let go of those people who makes you feel inferior. Why do you believe that there is no hope? Will you die because someone wants to make you strong by criticizing you? Was Bill Gate born with money? Was it not a Muslim that helps a Christian to succeed in school when his brothers and family failed him? Is Barrack Obama not an African yet the president of united state? Things change with time my friend. What is it that makes you feel worthless in life, that people has not face and overcome? My friend you are too precious to die, too important to be wasted, too beautiful to be ignored. Don't accept the lies of the devil that all is over, is not over yet because your victory is at hand. Don't settle for less I have come this far and have endure this much don't give up now. Commit your ways to God through praises and see the salvation of the lord.

A lady did it and her menstruation that was cease for 7 months was restored for just I hour of praise and worship. See! You that have thought of committing suicide as an option because of what you are going through, maybe resentments, abuse, lack and failure, I want to tell you that I have seen worst. Also understand that without battles there will be no victory. So if you die now where is the hero in you? Or will you say you don't want to be famous? Do you think that hero's are for special people or only for record breakers? No my friend, our situation is a hero in disguise. Handle it properly and you will see the hero in it, everyone wants to be a hero and here is your opportunity. Turn your life aright by making it count through letting people know how you turned your bad news to good news and become a legend of that situation. solving that solution by seeking God's help will launch you into a company of your own because people will certainly consult you when such problem of yours come to them and through it you will be known all over the world. Turn your situation into something amazing and be a hero of it. Problems are opportune to be hero's including yours. Testimonies have the power to reproduce it. And what are testimonies? Testimonies are solution to problems. Therefore without problems, there will be no miracles, testimonies or victories. Problems are raw material for greatness. Therefore see opportunity in your situation today and exploit them. Opportunities are not only in government, jobs, schooling abroad [oversea] but also in problems. All kinds of problems which your situation is part. Accept the opportunities and save a lot of youths by the testimonies of your life. If you give yourself a chance to solve those problems you will be certainly sure that you have save life because you are not the only one going through such situation. Others may be worse than yours but don't allow pride rob you your blessing because there is no place fill with honey or is there a place filled with gravel, nobody is too big or small but your choice is what matters in life. If God has used people to invent numerous things on earth which solves the most problems on earth, God is about using you to solve others. Note, before you can help others, you must know what to do. Therefore understand that it was only where your eyes can see that will be given to you. Abraham saw and it was given to him. **Gen.13v14-16And the LORD said unto Abram, after that Lot was separated from him, Lift up now thine eyes, and look from the place where thou art northward, and southward, and eastward, and westward: 15: For all the land which thou seest, to thee will I give it, and to thy seed for ever. 16: And I will make thy seed as the dust of the earth: so that if**

a man can number the dust of the earth, then shall thy seed also be numbered. if you sees beautiful things you will receive beautiful things. If Abraham has not seen it, it wouldn't have been possible for him to receive it from God. So until you see something, God is not permitted to bring it to pass and with your eyes shall you behold what God gives to you. Be only concern in the relationship you have with Christ other things are secondary because if you ask any thing in his name you will receive. **James4v2-7Ye lust, and have not: ye kill, and desire to have, and cannot obtain: ye fight and war, yet ye have not, because ye ask not. 3: Ye ask, and receive not, because ye ask amiss, that ye may consume it upon your lusts. 7 Submit yourselves therefore to God. Resist the devil, and he will flee from you.** A man ran into a road and was almost killed by a car and when been asked why such behavior? surprise he said I cannot rest in my house because of my wife. Some people are gift to others while other are grieve. Some find it very difficult to fix their marriage because they don't know who they really are before going into marriage and because they don't know,Satan takes advantage of it to destroy their marriage.

Marriage is sacrificing not entirely love. Remember that the two came from different background so don't expect 100% well from your spouse. I really don't know what it is that troubles you or that makes your life bitter but there is a solution to every problem of life and it is Jesus Christ the son of the living God and he is waiting to hear from you in prayers because he is willing to here all your problems and end everything that makes you cry. Spirituality is what advances you to supernatural happenings in your life, though you are made to be a solution not a problem but spirituality is what guarantees it. Understand that with the right spirituality heaven is your starting point, the sky is the limit of aircraft but to rocket its space, therefore receive the rocket dimension of grace as you obey and join the family of Christ.

Suicide is an act of foolishness mental confusion, problem and improper reasoning. Hey; Charles said its over between us, I cannot bear it anymore therefore I will jump into the river. They said am poor, I don't deserve to be in their midst therefore I will kill myself. See, this is negligence a whole me God I can't take it I will commit Suicide ...O what will people say about me? It's better to die than to lIve like this. No? There is no hope left for me in this earth, there is no reason to die live like. Brothers and sisters of great value, how can opportunity be misunderstood and mismanaged in our lives? How can we say we lack comfort when the Holy Ghost is always there for us? How can we say we lack money when 70% of Jesus parables are about business? Know that the road to success is discovering you. Is there any honorable way of dying in suicide? Is there any short cut to heaven? Why so you feel so worthless when you have the potentials that are being celebrated? It may not look like the time but it is true. Problems are first class opportunities, precious gifts to mankind to do exploits, why should we die for something that makes us better?

Life is not the problem why take lives as the problem? Whatever borders us is a problem therefore it is important to seek for a Godly way of solving lives problems than concluding that it is over, no hope! Every problem has a solution, nobody that has ever succeeded without trials and shame. There are two prices a man must pay in life, a price of pain and a price of gain.

You can't be blessed if you can't carry the blessings, no one teaches without knowing, and can't know without experience. Therefore understand that God is about to settle you

1peter5:10.

But the God of all grace, who hath called us unto his eternal glory by Christ Jesus, after that ye have suffered a while, make you perfect, stablish, strengthen, settle you.

So you are been strengthen for settlement. The level of your battles determines the level of your victories which is 20 sufferings equals 20 blessings. So expect a miracle in your situation. A friend of mine was telling me about life and at the end he said life is like a football team, a team loses match today and wins tomorrow but the secret of a successful match is that they (players) don't give up until 90 minute and additional time. Now in football its all about hiring and firing, a coach who was sacked in team A club goes to club B, a player that was rejected in club B goes to club A and win trophies, a player that was sacked in club B goes to club C and gets best player of the month. mourinho left Chelsea football club to inter Milan and won UEFA championship in Italy, Ancellotte was sacks at Chelsea but won UEFA championship with real Madrid of Spain. So that is how life is to us, it does not make Chelsea a bad club or inter Milan nor real Madrid a good club but time and chance happened to them all.

eccle 9:11

I returned, and saw under the sun, that the race is not to the swift, nor the battle to the strong, neither yet bread to the wise, nor yet riches to men of understanding, nor yet favour to men of skill; but time and chance happeneth to them all.

if Ancellotte had remained in Chelsea, he would not have won that trophy with real Madrid and Demato wouldn't have also won UEFA championship for Chelsea.

So understand that something must go for something to come, someone paid Shiloh sacrifice and was sacked from his only job that keeps him going but little did he know that it was a blessing and in the next 11 months he built his own house and bought two cars, where as he was at that job for 10 years and could not afford such growth. When Mourinho was asked to leave Chelsea, he would have probably felt bad but not knowing the mind of God that God wanted to reward his efforts at inter Milan. whatever might be your challenge don't give up on God, never hold on to anything tighter than you are holding onto God, because he cannot forget you. you have been long in your own ideas, try praising God today and see the result, don't be limited to the knowledge of your heart, try God today. When problems came for Ancellote and Mourinho they never gave up but moved on until they were celebrate in the end, you will be celebrated if you see opportunities in your situation and thinking of a way to exploit them rather than committing suicide. Problem solvers are people of value which means you are about to become a person of influence. We all have a choice to make but it's only a foolish man that takes his life himself, no matter the situation or circumstance because we don't own our life.

Thus for my part, more than once have i been broken in heart, I have been a parable to people and a total mockery before, everybody have bad times but after that i receive Jesus Christ my life changed and this book you are reading was also born through restoration of God promises in my life, I can't say much but I know that your problems are not as much that I survive from. What you might be facing today, might not be because of you alone but for some one that God wants you to be solution to because you are a solution to some ones problems so is every one. You have heard my advice, let me hear yours. The darkest hour is just before the dawn. This book is a product of my experiences in life, personal experiences. There is no true happiness without sadness. People add more values to their legs when they visit emergence ward in an hospital because a lots of legs are been hang, some are cut. Surely God will give you joy in that situation .rejoice for the days of your morning is over.

Suicide doesn't only involve or affect one person alone but also others. Envy is a barrier. Envy not your neighbors or friends for their success or vanities

prov23v17-18

Let not thine heart envy sinners: but be thou in the fear of the LORD all the day long.

18: For surely there is an end; and thine expectation shall not be cut off.

For envies has become a means in which devil use to destroy youths of today. Why jealous someone when you can do better. Wrong self belief is the destruction of the flesh and soul. Confidence in the wrong things is a divider of the heart. Lack of forgiveness is a burden, and hatred is heavier than a corpse. Always forgive and love

proverb.24v29

Say not, I will do so to him as he hath done to me: I will render to the man according to his work. There is no success without failure, when you don't know who you are in the LORD, abuse is inevitable, Problems are inevitable but there is confidence. Jesus Christ is our confidence in times of trouble. In the bible there were people that God turn their problems to favor. Joseph brothers actually wanted to kill him, but Reuben disagreed with them all and suggested they sell him into slavery. **Gen.37v13-19**

And Israel said unto Joseph, Do not thy brethren feed the flock in Shechem? come, and I will send thee unto them. And he said to him, Here am I.

14: And he said to him, Go, I pray thee, see whether it be well with thy brethren, and well with the flocks; and bring me word again. So he sent him out of the vale of Hebron, and he came to Shechem.

15: And a certain man found him, and, behold, he was wandering in the field: and the man asked him, saying, What seekest thou?

16: And he said, I seek my brethren: tell me, I pray thee, where they feed their flocks.

17: And the man said, They are departed hence; for I heard them say, Let us go to Dothan. And Joseph went after his brethren, and found them in Dothan.

18: And when they saw him afar off, even before he came near unto them, they conspired against him to slay him.

19: And they said one to another, Behold, this dreamer cometh. because of Joseph's dream and the love their father had for him. he was sold to the Ishmaelite trading on slavery, the Ishmaelite sold him to potiphar in Egypt **Gen. 37v36**

And the Midianites sold him into Egypt unto Potiphar, an officer of Pharaoh's, and captain of the guard.

then from potiphar's house to prison and from prison to palace. **Gen.41v14-37-44** remembers, Joseph was sold a slave, from slavery to prison and from prison he then became the prime minister in a foreign land.

Esther a Hebrew woman faced similar challenge when she heard of the decree of the king to kill and perish the Jews, Stirs up by Hanna

Esther 3v4-5

4:Now it came to pass, when they spake daily unto him, and he hearkened not unto them, that they told Haman, to see whether Mordecai's matters would stand: for he had told them that he was a Jew.

5:And when Haman saw that Mordecai bowed not, nor did him reverence, then was Haman full of wrath.

Finally the decree was reverse and the evil, plotted by Haman for mordecai bounced back at him and he was sentenced to death. Understand therefore that there is always a promotion attached to every problem in life.

Esther 6v10-12

10:Then the king said to Haman, Make haste, and take the apparel and the horse, as thou hast said, and do even so to Mordecai the Jew, that sitteth at the king's gate: let nothing fail of all that thou hast spoken.

11:Then took Haman the apparel and the horse, and arrayed Mordecai, and brought him on horseback through the street of the city, and proclaimed before him, Thus shall it be done unto the man whom the king delighteth to honour.

12: And Mordecai came again to the king's gate. But Haman hasted to his house mourning, and having his head covered. Mordecai was move from been at the kings gate to honor. Sometimes problems are always a part way to honor, if been treated in the right manner. David was a sheep keeper before God decided to uplift him by sending his servant Samuel the prophet to anoint him and after been anointed by Samuel a problem came that uplifted him.

1sam17v1-9

1:Now the Philistines gathered together their armies to battle, and were gathered together at Shochoh, which belongeth to Judah, and pitched between Shochoh and Azekah, in Ephesdammim. 2:And Saul and the men of Israel were gathered together, and pitched by the valley of Elah, and set the battle in array against the Philistines.

3: And the Philistines stood on a mountain on the one side, and Israel stood on a mountain on the other side: and there was a valley between them.

4: And there went out a champion out of the camp of the Philistines, named Goliath, of Gath, whose height was six cubits and a span.

5: And he had an helmet of brass upon his head, and he was armed with a coat of mail; and the weight of the coat was five thousand shekels of brass.

6: And he had greaves of brass upon his legs, and a target of brass between his shoulders.

7: And the staff of his spear was like a weaver's beam; and his spear's head weighed six hundred shekels of iron: and one bearing a shield went before him.

8: And he stood and cried unto the armies of Israel, and said unto them, Why are ye come out to set your battle in array? am not I a Philistine, and ye servants to Saul? choose you a man for you, and let him come down to me.

9: If he be able to fight with me, and to kill me, then will we be your servants: but if I prevail against him, and kill him, then shall ye be our servants, and serve us. David did not allow the height of goliath to intimidate him or his amours but was very confident of his God because he understood that victory is near

1sam.17v37

David said moreover, The LORD that delivered me out of the paw of the lion, and out of the paw of the bear, he will deliver me out of the hand of this Philistine. And Saul said unto David, Go, and the LORD be with thee.

And finally David defeated goliath and became a celebrity in such that even the king envied him. God has chosen David as the next king of Israel but God knew that he cannot be effective without building him up through troubles and trials. First David said **1sam17v36**

Thy servant slew both the lion and the bear: and this uncircumcised Philistine shall be as one of them, seeing he hath defied the armies of the living God.

Which means that even in sheep keeping there is lions and bears. Because he fought the lions and bears and even goliath, that was why he was able to defeat them and become a legend because of the confidence he has with God that was why he fought and was able to defeat them. Understand that whatever is worth fighting is worth wining. Therefore for an effective king to reign in any kingdom peacefully there must be battles, heart breaks, confusions, criticism and oppositions. So without pharaoh, there will be no more heroes. In **Ex.8v1**

And the LORD spake unto Moses, Go unto Pharaoh, and say unto him, Thus saith the LORD, Let my people go, that they may serve me.

Pharaoh let my people go was written several times in the bible and finally pharaoh let Israel go. It doesn't matter how many times you try solving a problem or how difficult the trouble seems only be persistent in everything, which is to the glory of God in your life. Remember that God allow Moses to go unto pharaoh several times to inform him that he should let go his people. Moses never seeks for ways of ending it at once but went bit by bit until pharaoh let the people of Israel go. Remember that no one that has ever done anything in a hurry does it right so stop being in a hurry to end your life because your love ones on earth will be heartbroken. Whatever that looks like pharaoh in your life must let you go in Jesus name Amen. And God grant the Israelites favor in the sight of the Egyptians that they came out with gold and silver and not with emptiness. So, will God do unto you in that ugly situation that troubles you in Jesus name Amen? Troubles and trails are opportunities to greater heights in life if the right knowledge is available. Daniel was in Babylon when the kings decree that any man or woman who did not bow to his gods will face a death sentence. But because Daniel was confident of his well able God he never bowed, so the king ordered that he being thrown into the lion's den,

(Dan. 6v26-28)

26: I make a decree, That in every dominion of my kingdom men tremble and fear before the God of Daniel: for he is the living God, and stedfast for ever, and his kingdom that which shall not be destroyed, and his dominion shall be even unto the end.

27: He delivereth and rescueth, and he worketh signs and wonders in heaven and in earth, who hath delivered Daniel from the power of the lions.

28: So this Daniel prospered in the reign of Darius, and in the reign of Cyrus the Persian.

that made the king of Babylon to know that there is a God in heaven that is most powerful than his gods. That was how his promotion came. And again Daniel interpreted the king's dream that made him a great man and governor over all the wise men of Babylon.

Daniel. 3v23-26

23 And these three men, Shadrach, Meshach, and Abednego, fell down bound into the midst of the burning fiery furnace.

24 Then Nebuchadnezzar the king was astonied, and rose up in haste, and spake, and said unto his counsellors, Did not we cast three men bound into the midst of the fire? They answered and said unto the king, True, O king.

25 He answered and said, Lo, I see four men loose, walking in the midst of the fire, and they have no hurt; and the form of the fourth is like the Son of God.

26: Then Nebuchadnezzar came near to the mouth of the burning fiery furnace, and spake, and said, Shadrach, Meshach, and Abednego, ye servants of the most high God, come forth, and come hither. Then Shadrach, Meshach, and Abednego, came forth of the midst of the fire.

Therefore let people know how you solve problems, and also become a person of value because people with similar challenge will do what you did to gain victory in whatever situation they are passing through in life. The 3 Hebrew boys in **(Dan.3)** which are shedrach, Meshach and Abednego. Who were cast into the burning fiery furnace was promoted.

By the same king that threw them into the furnace so there is promotions in problems. Whatever you are going through is a part way to your success. And in case you don't believe in God the owner of the universe, the alpha and omega, Jehovah, the beginning and the end, Jesus Christ the son of the living God, and you don't believe in the word of God written in the word of God that God created you and wishes good for you as told in **3john2** consider football coaches sacked here and with trophy here. Why persistence, therefore be persistence in everything good in your life whether it looks possible or not just keep trying, Job that was battered in affliction was letter blessed in double portion.

Job 42: 10

And the LORD turned the captivity of Job, when he prayed for his friends: also the LORD gave Job twice as much as he had before.

Therefore rejoice because you are about to be double in blessing don't lose it. I pray the LORD bless you and keep you, the LORD make his face shine upon you and be gracious unto you. The LORD lifts his countenance upon you and gives you peace amen.

Chapter 5

IMMORALITY

ECCLESIASTES 12:13-14

I realize that many youths of today does not have this knowledge of the fear of God and keep his commandments because this is the whole duty of man. for the lack of this knowledge, many has died unfulfilled, some lost some parts of their body and some perpetually remained sick.

Youths are the leaders of tomorrow and whereby they fail as a result of lack of the thorough knowledge of GOD, the whole earth fails. Therefore I will not have you ignorant of this very fact that the Lord of glory been Jesus Christ have better thoughts for everyone us that is join to the living.

JEREMIAH 29:11

For I know the thoughts that I think toward you, saith the LORD, thoughts of peace, and not of evil, to give you an expected end.

From the research, I have found that everything God told man to do is for his own good whether he said do or don't do is for his own good. What then is IMMORALITY? According to oxford advance learners dictionary immorality is not following accepted standards of morality. Then what is morality? by the same dictionary, morality means principles concerning right and wrong or good and bad behaviors. What then are the principles of God? That is the right and wrong of him? In the book of

Exodus 20:12-17

Honour thy father and thy mother: that thy days may be long upon the land which the LORD thy God giveth thee.

13: Thou shalt not kill.

14: Thou shalt not commit adultery.

15: Thou shalt not steal.

16: Thou shalt not bear false witness against thy neighbour.

17: Thou shalt not covet thy neighbour's house, thou shalt not covet thy neighbour's wife, nor his manservant, nor his maidservant, nor his ox, nor his ass, nor any thing that is thy neighbour's.

These are other principles that we will be looking at that is not mention in the verse.

- Adultery/fornication
- Assault and battery
- Rape
- Seduction
- Oppression
- Kidnapping
- Slander

1. *ADULTERY/ FORNICATION*

Adultery and fornication are the same only that adultery is the elder brother of fornication.

The bible said in

1 COR 6:9-19

9: Know ye not that the unrighteous shall not inherit the kingdom of God? Be not deceived: neither fornicators, nor idolaters, nor adulterers, nor effeminate, nor abusers of themselves with mankind, 19: Flee fornication. Every sin that a man doeth is without the body; but he that committeth fornication sinneth against his own body.

Adultery has curse a lot of pains in the family today; adultery has brought sickness upon families and other things. 60% of divorce rate is caused by adultery because it is an act of betrayal which sometimes brings hatred. Hatred comes in, it gives birth to misunderstanding or rather misbehavior and at the end divorce becomes the solution and if this family has children they become the victims. Because is either they lack fatherly care or love or even presence or they lack motherly presence. Therefore the act of adultery is to the expense of the children. And if a father loves his family he should have no reason to do this because is like destroying what he spent twenty year to build in twenty minutes.

Fornication in order hand is widely known or accepted in the world. Pornography film has made it very easy for people to practice fornication. Fornication now in some area is no longer a sin but a proper thing in fact if a girl says that she is a virgin people will mock her by saying that she lack 0pportunity in fact there is a tribe in Nigeria according to what I read that when friend visits his friend for the first time, for the night the man will give his friend to his wife for the night to them it is a sign of appreciating his friend.

Another tribe before marriage, gives his propose wife to his brother to take to bed and see how active she is on bed and that will determine whether he will go on or not. invariably making adultery or fornication a way of life. Pornography films, the use of internet in phones has promoted fornication so much that even a child of eight years knows what fornication is all about. Remember that the bible said flee from fornication according to the book of **Matthew 5:27-28,**

27: Ye have heard that it was said by them of old time, Thou shalt not commit adultery:

28: But I say unto you, That whosoever looketh on a woman to lust after her hath committed adultery with her already in his heart.

DEUTERONOMY 5:18

Neither shalt thou commit adultery.

Please note that fornication is a spirit and when the spirit is upon someone, it is difficult to control but not impossible because with God all things are possible.

LUKE 1:37

For with God nothing shall be impossible.

Therefore I pray for everyone under the influence of the spirit of fornication to be liberated in Jesus name Amen

Fornication has curse several pains in the lives of the youths today because through fornication is unwanted pregnancies, through fornication is sickness, through fornication is death (abortion) through fornication is hindrance from God, through fornication has youths or humans lost a lot of things. Therefore I beseech you to flee from it or marry if it be the best part. Fornication brings rape cases and no father will want his child to be rape. For several rape cases was as a result of people not been able to control fornication.

OPPRESSION:

The poor is despite even in his own land. I observe this in different places I have been especially in Africa and all over the world though is an individual thing because I have seen a family that oppress a maid but one was kind and very loving to him. that oppression has been the order of the day. But what is God saying about the matter.

In the book of **EXODUS 22; 21-24**

21: Thou shalt neither vex a stranger, nor oppress him: for ye were strangers in the land of Egypt.

22: Ye shall not afflict any widow, or fatherless child.

23: If thou afflict them in any wise, and they cry at all unto me, I will surely hear their cry;

24: And my wrath shall wax hot, and I will kill you with the sword; and your wives shall be widows, and your children fatherless.

Oppression is growing rapidly now in Africa and in Nigeria and some places of employment where the employer treats the employee as if he or she is a no body. I write this because the bible condemns oppression and I have seen it around me here and how it make people look small. I don't know if this is largely found in Europe where an employer refuses to pay his employee just because he feels that whether or not they can do him no harm.

DEUTERONOMY 24:14-18

14: Thou shalt not oppress an hired servant that is poor and needy, whether he be of thy brethren, or of thy strangers that are in thy land within thy gates:

15: At his day thou shalt give him his hire, neither shall the sun go down upon it; for he is poor, and setteth his heart upon it: lest he cry against thee unto the LORD, and it be sin unto thee.

16: The fathers shall not be put to death for the children, neither shall the children be put to death for the fathers: every man shall be put to death for his own sin.

17: Thou shalt not pervert the judgment of the stranger, nor of the fatherless; nor take a widow's raiment to pledge:

18: But thou shalt remember that thou wast a bondman in Egypt, and the LORD thy God redeemed thee thence: therefore I command thee to do this thing.

Please understand that everyone was created under the image of god and all is the children of the Most High God. Therefore no matter the color or language let there be no oppression

SEDUCTION:

As I early said, if you are not in Christ, you are in crisis because you are open to the devil to manipulate. Seduction has been a vice which the devil uses to carry out his wicked deeds. A Holy Spirit filled man of God will be counseling a girl before you know what happens, she tries seducing him. to this end, Some pastors has learned to keep their office door open to avoid such misbehavior. seduction is in many forms, some are to create an atmosphere of destruction especially to pastors and people of God and Some to archive their lust over something they desired.

But the bible said in **REV 2:20-22**. …To seduce my servants to commit fornication. Married men nowadays seduce young girls with their big and expensive cars and money just to commit fornication. These men sometimes go for both someone that cannot be up to the age of their daughter. These men do this because they believe that they have the money and they can do anything moreover the girls need their money to help themselves in their schools or meet the demands of life.

But all these is at the expense of the girls because it is a sin and her future is at stake because if anything happens, that money cannot do anything and the man will run away then she alone bears the pains. Even the man can go to the extent of killing her to hide it from his family. Then what is the gain of going out with someone that is ashamed of you? Seduction is immorality.

2Timothy 3:6-8

6: For of this sort are they which creep into houses, and lead captive silly women laden with sins, led away with divers lusts,

7: Ever learning, and never able to come to the knowledge of the truth.

8: Now as Jannes and Jambres withstood Moses, so do these also resist the truth: men of corrupt minds, reprobate concerning the faith.

Also in

2Timothy2:22

Flee also youthful lusts: but follow righteousness, faith, charity, peace, with them that call on the Lord out of a pure heart.

I have known that everything that happens on earth has a spiritual backing therefore there is a spirit behind seduction. That is why some churches in Nigeria don't allow ladies to seat in front of the church. Please note that ladies are not the carriers of this spirit but it is visibly seen in some of them. Especially when the devil wants to put enmity between God and man through fornication.

Finally immorality is against the status of God. Take a country as an example if the law of the country is don't steal and the person steals will not the person be judged? And if proven guilty won't he pay for it?

But god is not so, the bible says in **DEUTERONOMY 4; 29-31**

29: But if from thence thou shalt seek the LORD thy God, thou shalt find him, if thou seek him with all thy heart and with all thy soul.

30: When thou art in tribulation, and all these things are come upon thee, even in the latter days, if thou turn to the LORD thy God, and shalt be obedient unto his voice;

31: (For the LORD thy God is a merciful God;) he will not forsake thee, neither destroy thee, nor forget the covenant of thy fathers which he sware unto them.

Also he said in

Jeremiah 3:13-15

13: Only acknowledge thine iniquity, that thou hast transgressed against the LORD thy God, and hast scattered thy ways to the strangers under every green tree, and ye have not obeyed my voice, saith the LORD.

14: Turn, O backsliding children, saith the LORD; for I am married unto you: and I will take you one of a city, and two of a family, and I will bring you to Zion:

15: And I will give you pastors according to mine heart, which shall feed you with knowledge and understanding.

Therefore friends acknowledge him now and are free from all oppressions of the devil

I pray that the mercies of God be with you now and always in Jesus name Amen

Printed in the United States
By Bookmasters